W9-CDZ-135

AMSTERDAM
ENCOUNTER

ZORA O'NEILL

Amsterdam Encounter

Published by Lonely Planet Publications Pty Ltd

ABN 36 005 607 983

Australia	Head Office, Locked Bag 1, Footscray, Victoria 3011 ☎ 03 8379 8000 fax 03 8379 8111 talk2us@lonelyplanet.com.au
USA	150 Linden St, Oakland, CA 94607 ☎ 510 250 6400 toll free 800 275 8555 fax 510 893 8572 info@lonelyplanet.com
UK	2nd fl, 186 City Rd, London EC1V 2NT ☎ 020 7106 2100 fax 020 7106 2101 go@lonelyplanet.co.uk

This title was commissioned in Lonely Planet's London office and produced by: **Commissioning Editor** Caroline Sieg **Coordinating Editor** Katie O'Connell **Coordinating Cartographer** Julie Dodkins **Layout Designer** Cara Smith **Managing Editor** Lauren Hunt **Managing Cartographer** Mark Griffiths **Managing Layout Designer** Laura Jane **Assisting Editor** Simone Egger **Assisting Cartographers** Fatima Basic, James Regan **Cover Designer** Dan Baird **Project Managers** Chris Girdler, Craig Kilburn **Series Designer** Mik Ruff **Thanks to** Imogen Bannister, Andrea Beattie, Adam Bextream, Barbara Delissen, Lisa Knights, Wayne Murphy, Trent Paton, Jacqui Saunders, Rob van Brevoort

ISBN 978 1 74104 990 9

Printed by Hang Tai Printing Company.
Printed in China.

Acknowledgement Amsterdam Transport Network Map © GVB Amsterdam.

HOW TO USE THIS BOOK
Colour-Coding & Maps

Colour-coding is used for symbols on maps and in the text that they relate to (eg all eating venues on the maps and in the text are given a green knife and fork symbol). Each neighbourhood also gets its own colour, and this is used down the edge of the page and throughout that neighbourhood section.

Shaded yellow areas on the maps denote 'areas of interest' – for their historical significance, their attractive architecture or their great bars and restaurants. We encourage you to head to these areas and just start exploring!

Prices

Multiple prices listed with reviews (eg €10/5 or €10/5/20) indicate adult/child, adult/concession or adult/child/family.

Send us your feedback We love to hear from readers – your comments help make our books better. We read every word you send us, and we always guarantee that your feedback goes straight to the appropriate authors. The most useful submissions are rewarded with a free book. To send us your updates and find out about Lonely Planet events, newsletters and travel news visit our award-winning website: **lonelyplanet.com/contact**

Note: We may edit, reproduce and incorporate your comments in Lonely Planet products such as guidebooks, websites and digital products, so let us know if you don't want your comments reproduced or your name acknowledged. For a copy of our privacy policy visit **lonelyplanet.com/privacy**.

ZORA O'NEILL

Fresh out of college, Zora O'Neill arrived in
Amsterdam to work at a cafe adjoining a scrappy
improv theatre (now the comedy juggernaut
Boom Chicago; p92). Her job description called
for dispensing tourist advice along with grilled
sandwiches – a bit flawed, considering she'd just
arrived herself. If you got lost looking for that
'super easy-to-find' bike route to Marken in 1994,
Zora's very sorry. Fortunately, she's much more
qualified now; with in-laws, friends and her own
bike in Amsterdam, she visits every year. The first
thing she does when she arrives is eat a *broodje*

haring (p89), and the second thing she does is get on a boat. The rest of
the year, she lives in Astoria, Queens, where she writes about food and
travel. She has been a guidebook author since 2003; this is her second
book for Lonely Planet.

ZORA'S THANKS

Many thanks to Constant Broeren, Bas Bruijn, Edwin Oppedijk, Mark
Morse, Rod Ben Zeev, Lieselotte Nooyen and Binkie Dabekaussen. I'm
grateful to my interviewees for giving me a new perspective on the city,
to all my Amsterdam friends who shared their best secrets, and to Peter,
for steering the boat. At Lonely Planet, thanks to Caroline Sieg, who did
some steering herself, and to Jeremy Gray, author of the previous Lonely
Planet guide to Amsterdam.

Our readers Many thanks to the travellers who wrote to us with helpful hints, useful advice and interesting
anecdotes: Brian Beveridge, Shoaban Nair, Charlotte Nikolaeva, Ophelia Rubinich, Tzach Sarid, Aulene Wessel,
Angela Williams.

Cover photograph Cyclist crossing a bridge in the heart of Amsterdam's canal belt © Formcourt / Alamy.
Internal photographs p22, p24, p157, p159 Netherlands Board of Tourism & Conventions; p21, p156 Eduard
Bergman (NTBC); p49, p71, p87, p107 by Zora O'Neill. All other photographs by Lonely Planet Images, and by Will
Salter except p8 Christian Aslund; p4 Paul Beinssen; p28 Simon Foale; p40, p52, p64, p94, p98, p116, p118, p141
Martin Moos; p11, 165 Richard Nebesky; p36 Zaw Min Yu.

All images are copyright of the photographers unless otherwise indicated. Many of the images in this guide are
available for licensing from **Lonely Planet Images:** www.lonelyplanetimages.com.

On your bike: take to the streets on two wheels, in one of the world's most cycle-friendly cities

CONTENTS

THIS IS AMSTERDAM

You're sitting on a small boat, sliding along the curve of the Prinsengracht. It's twilight, and the sky is painted the richest indigo. The white lights edging the canal bridges reflect on the black water, and the windows in the gabled houses glow gold.

It's just another gorgeous evening in Amsterdam, a magical city where 17th-century buildings lean against each other like fond old friends, and the mindset of residents is one of the most progressive in the world.

Amsterdam may be famous for its pragmatic approach to sex and drugs, but once you're here for more than an afternoon, you'll see how this policy fits right into a city that values its inhabitants' rights to pursue their interests – whether that means opening a shop specialising in toothbrushes or skating around town in nothing but a rhinestone-studded jockstrap.

It is true that Amsterdammers will take any excuse to party till dawn, and concert halls and clubs are booked solid with entertainment from all over the globe. Combine this with a flourishing design scene and catwalk style during the biannual fashion week, and it's hard to believe that Amsterdam is a city of only 750,000 people.

It is growing though, as you'll see from the construction scaffolding visible all over town. With a new metro line being laid and a harbour that seems to sprout a fresh architectural marvel every month, this metropolis is in fast-forward motion. Earlier in the decade, fiery national debates, two high-profile murders and protests over immigration caused citywide anxiety. But Amsterdammers are too relaxed to live in crisis mode for long; they've now gotten back to business, settled into their beloved candlelit bars, flocked to the clubs – or donned their wigs and platform boots and hopped back on their bicycles. In short, they're still doing their own thing. Care to join in? Just pack a few days' attitude, and climb aboard.

Top left Getting into the swing of things at the Dampkring coffeeshop (p53) **Top right** The sun sets on Groenburgwal canal in the heart of the Southern Canal Belt **Bottom** A motorcyclist pauses outside Koninklijk Paleis (p42)

Orange-clad Amsterdammers celebrate Koninginnedag (Queen's Day; p23) every 30 April

>1 RIJKSMUSEUM

MASTER THE OLD MASTERS AT THE RIJKSMUSEUM

The Rijksmuseum (p98) is the Netherlands' treasure house, established when the country was one of the wealthiest in the world. It has grown into a collection of more than a million objects of art, including 5000 paintings, which represent the artists of the Dutch Golden Age as well as notable works from elsewhere in Europe. Pending completion of the monumental 1885 building's renovation in 2012, currently only a small portion of the treasures are on view in a side wing. Hardcore art-lovers will be a bit disappointed, but in many ways this limited selection, which takes about two hours to see, is a very manageable treat.

All the greatest hits are here, including portraits by Frans Hals, rowdy pub scenes by Jan Steen, domestic tableaux by Johannes Vermeer and the glowing cows that Paulus Potter specialised in. If you're lucky, you'll also see Jan Asselijn's malevolent swan – but the exact selections, which might also include examples of fine delftware and some of the 17th- and 18th-century dollhouses the museum owns, change a few times a year. One work, though, is always on display – Rembrandt's *The Night Watch*, a strikingly luminous work that broke new ground in the field of civic guards' portraits.

>2 ANNE FRANK HUIS

VISIT ANNE FRANK'S SECRET ANNEXE

Young Anne Frank would have been another anonymous victim of the Holocaust, were it not for her illuminating diary, written during the two years she and her family lived hidden in the back of her father's offices with another family attempting to avoid Nazi persecution. Translated into some 60 languages and adapted as a stage play and film, her writing reflects all the travails of an ordinary teenage girl, unable to swim against the tide of extraordinary times. The hidden families were eventually revealed to the Gestapo, and Anne died in Bergen-Belsen concentration camp just months before the war ended.

The focus of the Anne Frank Huis (p62) is the *achterhuis* (rear house), the secret annexe behind a revolving bookcase. It was in this dark and airless space that the Franks observed complete silence during the day, outgrew their clothes, pasted photos of Hollywood stars on the walls and read Dickens, before being mysteriously betrayed and sent to their deaths. The claustrophobic rooms, their windows still covered with blackout screens, are bare of furniture at the request of Anne's father Otto, the only member of the group to survive the camps. But poignant traces are still visible – the children's heights marked on the door frame, for instance. The house has been a museum since 1957, and now incorporates a modern wing that addresses issues of present-day racism and anti-Semitism.

>3 DE WALLEN

GET AN EYEFUL IN THE RED-LIGHT DISTRICT

As much as the tourism board wishes it weren't so, the district called De Wallen (The Quays) is a distinguishing feature of Amsterdam. Perhaps what's most fascinating about the red-light district is that it's not a festering den of sleaze. Granted, lads on lost weekends don't set a great tone, but this may be the safest vice zone in the world. De Wallen is a functioning neighbourhood, complete with kids, older residents, cosy cafes and postcard-worthy canals.

To the Dutch, legal prostitution is simply common sense, as is, for that matter, the marijuana sold at the 'coffeeshops' that alternate with the pubs, sex shops and peep-show theatres. But it's still mind-bending when you first set eyes on the women in the windows, illuminated not only with red lights, but also with black ones that make their white lingerie glow enticingly. (Your first instinct might be to take a photo, but don't do it – out of simple respect, and to avoid having your camera tossed in a canal by the ladies' enforcers.)

Go first in the midmorning, when the neighbourhood is waking up: prostitutes on the early shift chat out their windows as grannies go out for a stroll. Stop in at De Bakkerswinkel (p47) or Hofje van Wijs (p48) for a pastry and a *koffie verkeerd* (milky coffee), and visit the beautiful Oude Kerk (p43), the city's oldest house of worship. Take a tour at the Prostitution Information Centre (p43), and finish with a shot of *jenever* (Dutch-style gin) at Wijnand Fockink (p56).

Come back in the evening, when all the neon lights are on, and

RED MEANS STOP?

In early 2008 the city government announced it wanted to 'restore the balance' in De Wallen, citing too much influence of organised crime in prostitution and coffeeshops. To encourage entrepreneurs to invest in cleaner businesses in the area, the city is acting as a guarantor for investors to buy brothel buildings. Firm plans for the properties won't be decided until 2009 – 'but it won't involve McDonald's or Starbucks', one city official assured us. Visitors probably won't see the effects of the project for several years, but it shouldn't mean the end of the red-light windows altogether.

edge down the city's narrowest alley, the metre-wide Trompetters-teeg, lined with red-light windows (look for the entrance in the block south of the Oude Kerk). Maybe take in a live sex show at Casa Rosso (p57), or just head to one of the many nonexplicit nightspots, like Winston Kingdom (p57) or In 't Aepjen (p55).

It's worth noting that this isn't the only red-light district in Amsterdam – there's another stretch of windows on Spuistraat, and some on Ruysdaelkade in De Pijp. Likewise, there are coffeeshops all over the city as well (see p161). But nowhere else has quite the stimulating mix of history and industry as De Wallen.

>4 NEGEN STRAATJES

SHOP 'TIL YOU DROP ON THE 'NINE LITTLE STREETS'

In a city packed with shopping opportunities, the Negen Straatjes represent the very densest concentration of consumer pleasures. These nine streets are indeed quite small, each one a block long. They form a grid connecting the three main canals in the Western Canal Belt, south of Raadhuisstraat. The shops here are also quite small, and many are highly specialised. For velvet ribbons, visit HJ van de Kerkhof (p66); for toothbrushes, De Witte Tanden Winkel (p65); for single-edition art books, Boekie Woekie (p64). It's also the place to head for fashion: edgy Belgian and Dutch designers at Van Ravenstein (p68), eye-popping shoes at Hester van Eeghen (p65), or vintage treasures at Laura Dols (p67). This book would sink under the weight of all the delightful shops, so we've included only a handful and left the rest for you to discover (extra points if you find the doll doctor!).

After zigzagging through even a portion of the streets, you'll probably need some rejuvenation – no problem, because there are plenty of cafes in the Negen Straatjes as well. Snack in chic surrounds at Wolvenstraat (p77), or enjoy the peace and quiet at De Pels (p74). Note that shopkeepers in the Negen Straatjes like to relax too – many are closed entirely on Monday, and sometimes Tuesday, so plan your grand tour for later in the week.

>5 DUTCH DESIGN

SOLVE DESIGN PROBLEMS YOU DIDN'T KNOW YOU HAD

Built on piles sunk deep in a bog and cut through with serene canals, the whole city of Amsterdam is an elegant design solution. So it's no surprise that Dutch design has a reputation for creative approaches to everyday objects. A few big names – Hella Jongerius, Gijs Bakker and Marcel Wanders – are known internationally, but true to inclusive Amsterdam form, the best work often comes out of collectives such as Droog (p126), where member designers needn't be Dutch – they just need to think as if they are, and have a knack for repurposing, reinventing and sometimes just laughing. Droog's signature designs employ surreal humour (a chandelier made of 80-plus light bulbs clustered like fish eggs) as well as practicality, as in the off-centre umbrella, surely inspired by the country's weather.

Dutch designers take a cock-eyed look at their own heritage too. At Amsterdam's temple of home decor, Frozen Fountain (p65), you can see tongue-in-cheek versions of delftware and traditional textiles. But gems from the past are treasured at Bebob Design (p85), Wonderwood (p47) and other vintage specialists.

The stereotypically thrifty Dutch love a well-designed bargain too. All-purpose shop HEMA (p45) has developed a cult following by commissioning design students to put a spin on everything from espresso cups to handbags. Once you have a hand towel with a rivet in one corner for hanging, you'll wonder how you lived without it!

>6 BICYCLES

TAKE TO THE CITY ON TWO WHEELS

With the possible exception of Copenhagen, no other city in the world is quite as bicycle-mad as Amsterdam. Dutch riders see their two-wheeled transport as nothing special, but one of the greatest sights for visitors is the sheer diversity of the city's bicycles. Among the estimated 600,000 bikes in the city, you'll spot everything from the standard curvy black *omafiets* (granny bike) to flashy customised jobs trimmed with plastic flowers. Mums load toddlers in the front bins of their *bakfietsen* (cargo bikes) or stack the kids on front and back seats. Hip youngsters in teensy skirts arrive at nightclubs on bikes, and bankers zip off to work on theirs, ties flapping in the breeze.

By far the best way to appreciate Amsterdam's bicycle-friendliness is to ride one yourself. They're available for rent all over (see p175 for a couple of recommended companies), and once you're up and rolling, you'll see the city from a whole new angle, shoulder to shoulder with local commuters on the 400km of dedicated cycle paths. It's worth devoting a day to near-aimless cycling – pick one relatively distant sight, like the Tropenmuseum (p113) or the cool architecture of the Eastern Docklands (p132), and let yourself get lost on your way there. Once you have a taste of the freedom a bike affords, you won't want to give it up.

>7 CANALS

MAKE A DATE WITH AMSTERDAM'S WATERWAYS

To say Amsterdammers love the water is an understatement. Sure, the city made its first fortune in maritime trade, but that's ancient history. Here in the present, on a sunny Sunday afternoon, you can see the local aquaphilia just by sitting canalside and watching the boats go by. Some cafes – such as Het Molenpad (p74) and 't Smalle (p76) – seem purpose-built for this sport. Or you could stroll next to the canals and check out some of the city's 3300 houseboats. The Prinsengracht is lined with a particularly great mix of homes, from mod blocks to cobbled-together creations, and you can even tour one at the Houseboat Museum (p62).

Definitely make time in your schedule for a canal tour (p178). If it's raining, you'll have to take one of the giant glassed-in boats, but if it's clear, hop aboard a smaller open-air operation and feel the wind in your hair. A short (and free) ferry ride (p174) across the IJ harbour gives you a taste of the industrial side of Amsterdam's watery heritage – and if you like that, you can dine on a boat as well (p51).

From boat level you'll get to see a whole new set of architectural details, like the ornamentation on all the bridges. And when you pass the canalside cafe terraces, you can just look up and wave.

>8 VONDELPARK

LAZE AROUND IN VONDELPARK – CAN YOU DIG IT?

As integral to Amsterdam as the canals and cafes, Vondelpark (p99) is the place to be on a sunny day. The long, narrow park was laid out as a green belt for the Amsterdam elite in the 1860s, and named after the poet and playwright Joost van den Vondel (the Shakespeare of the Dutch language). But the rambling green space has been thoroughly democratised since then, thanks in part to the hippies who camped here en masse in the summer of 1970.

As representatives of every thread of Amsterdam's social fabric descend, a party atmosphere ensues. Some people kick back by reading a book, some cradle a beer at one of the cafes, some share a spliff and strum songs on the guitar. Street performers work the crowds and kids rush the playgrounds. The atmosphere is so anything-goes, in fact, that the city council will probably have legalised anonymous sex in the infamous cruising area of the rose gardens (but only after dark, and then visitors must be sure to pick up after themselves) by the time you read this. On the other hand, full nudity is banned, though plenty of people strip off their tops to work on their tans. Ponds, lawns and winding footpaths encourage visitors to explore. Keep your eyes and ears open – you might hear an organ concert or see a flock of parakeets.

>9 ALBERT CUYPMARKT

SNACK YOUR WAY THROUGH A STREET MARKET

You *could* go to the half-mile-long Albert Cuypmarkt (p106) to buy pink plastic sandals, a whole fish, a bike lock or cheap lingerie. You could also go to marvel at Amsterdam in all its diversity, as the century-old market is in the middle of a neighbourhood known for its immigrant roots. Stalls cater to Surinamese, Moroccan and Indonesian clientele, and to cheese-lovers wherever they may hail from. Vendors loudly tout their odd gadgets and their stupendous arrays of fresh fruit.

But we wouldn't want you to get distracted by the scene and overlook the snacks. Certainly you can get *frites* (French or, more correctly, Belgian fries) from a few stands along the route, but you can also savour some other essential culinary titbits the Dutch hold dear. Start your lunch with a *broodje haring* – raw herring on a soft bun, topped with sweet pickles (for more on this treat, see the boxed text on p89). Then tuck into a fresh-fried *loempia*, a crispy miniature egg roll that entered Dutch culinary tradition via Indonesia – make sure you don't forget the sweet-hot sauce. For dessert, track down the *stroopwafel* man, who doles out thin cookies stuck together with caramel, hot off a dedicated griddle. You can smell the cinnamon from a block away.

>10 VAN GOGH MUSEUM

APPRECIATE THE NETHERLANDS' MOST TORTURED ARTIST AT THE VAN GOGH MUSEUM

Visiting this vast collection of canvases by Vincent van Gogh (1853–90) is as much a tour through the driven painter's troubled mind as it is a tour through his body of work. More than 200 paintings are arranged chronologically, starting with his early career in dreary old Holland – and sombre, depressive paintings like *The Potato Eaters* – and ending less than a decade later in sunny Arles, where he produced his best-known work with his characteristic giddy, intense colour. Van Gogh committed suicide in 1890 at the age of 37 (not long after famously cutting off his own ear during a dispute with Paul Gauguin), and he sold only one painting in his lifetime.

The museum opened in 1973 to house Theo van Gogh's collection of his brother's paintings, drawings and sketchbooks, and some 800 letters written by the artist. These are complemented by a small selection of paintings by contemporaries, most of whom were friends, such as Toulouse-Lautrec and Gauguin, or artists he admired, such as Jean-François Millet. This is all laid out in a blocky building by premier Dutch architect Gerrit Rietveld, and the museum also hosts superb temporary exhibitions in a separate Kisho Kurokawa–designed wing (dubbed 'The Mussel' by locals). See p98 for more information.

>AMSTERDAM DIARY

Understandably for such a rain-sodden city, the busiest time for festivals in Amsterdam is July and August, when performers have the best chance of clear skies. In autumn (September to November), the regular cultural season starts up at the established venues and runs through to spring (March to May). January and February are slow in terms of formal events, but there are only-in-winter perks like ice skating at Museumplein (p96) and hot-chocolate stands around town. For a schedule of events during your visit, pick up a copy of the city tourist board's monthly *Day by Day* or an issue of *Amsterdam Weekly*, also online at www.amsterdamweekly.com.

Spectators gather on the city's harbour during Sail Amsterdam (p24)

JANUARY

Amsterdam International Fashion Week

www.aifw.nl

Amsterdam's fledgling fashion scene takes flight with events around the city, but primarily based at Westergasfabriek. Unlike many fashion weeks, there's a substantial program open to the public.

FEBRUARY

Februaristaking

A commemoration of the dock workers' strike of 25 February 1941, to protest the German occupation and the persecution of Jews. There's a ceremony at the *Dokwerker* statue next to the Portuguese-Israelite Synagogue (p124).

MARCH

Stille Omgang

www.stille-omgang.nl, in Dutch

Some 9000 people attend this silent march commemorating the Miracle of Amsterdam of 1354 (see p41).

APRIL

Amsterdam Fantastic Film Festival

www.afff.nl

Horror, sci-fi, anime and more crowd the screen at this 11-day genre-fest. Best of all, it's at the gorgeous Tuschinskitheater (p85).

World Press Photo

www.worldpressphoto.org

This gripping display of the year's best photojournalism debuts in the Oude Kerk in late April, and stays on display until June.

Tune in to the city's heartbeat on Koninginnedag (Queen's Day)

Koninginnedag

Queen's Day, April 30, is a celebration of the House of Orange, with more than 400,000 orange-clad people filling Amsterdam's streets for drinking and dancing. The city also becomes one big flea market, as people sell off all their unwanted junk.

MAY

Art Amsterdam

www.artamsterdam.nl

Formerly known as KunstRAI, this international art fair draws buyers with deep pockets – it's chic and commercial.

Kunstvlaai

www.kunstvlaai.nl

What used to be a fringe version of Art Amsterdam is now a standalone event, with some overlapping dates. Expect odd installations, open studios and more.

JUNE

Holland Festival

www.hollandfestival.nl

The winter culture season winds up with a bang at this big-name theatre, dance and opera festival – it acts as the bookend to Uitmarkt (p25).

Amsterdam Roots Festival

www.amsterdamroots.nl

Fantastic world music programming at several big venues for five days, plus free concerts in Oosterpark (p113), in one of the city's most diverse neighbourhoods.

Open Tuinen Dagen

www.opentuinendagen.nl

Grand homes on the canal belt open their gardens to visitors for one weekend near the end of the month.

JULY

5 Days Off

www.5daysoff.nl, in Dutch

Electronic music gets its due at this fest in the major club venues. The programming is edgier and more selective than Amsterdam Dance Event (p25), and the feeling more intimate.

Over Het IJ

www.overhetij.nl

The raw industrial space of the NDSM shipyards is the setting for this equally raw theatre festival. Take the ferry over and prepare to be delighted – many of the shows are physical, or in English.

Amsterdam International Fashion Week

www.aifw.nl

The summer edition of the city's fashion festivities (opposite).

Julidans
www.julidans.nl

For the entire month, Amsterdam's substantial modern dance scene is on show – along with international guests – at the city's biggest venues.

Kwakoe
www.kwakoe.nl, in Dutch

Every weekend in July, this massive food-and-football fair celebrates Surinamese culture. Its future was hazy in 2008 – but it's worth the trip to the Bijlmer if it continues.

AUGUST

Amsterdam Pride
www.amsterdampride.nl

The last weekend in July or the first in August is dedicated to this completely over-the-top gay fest, with a parade on the canals followed by street parties.

De Parade
www.deparade.nl, in Dutch

This cool short-performance theatre fest takes place in a collection of circus tents in Martin Luther King Park. It runs nightly for the first half of the month, and usually includes a lot of physical, non-language-dependent shows.

Sail Amsterdam
www.sail2010.nl, in Dutch

Sail is a massive once-every-five-years convention of the world's great tall ships.

Y-M-C-A: Take to the canals during Pride

Amsterdam's harbour, crowded with masts, is a beautiful vision of yesteryear. The next event is 19–23 August 2010.

Grachtenfestival
www.grachtenfestival.nl

Classical music takes to the water in this eight-day festival. The highlight is the free concert on a barge opposite the Pulitzer hotel, attended by nearly every boat in the city.

Hartjesdag

A cross-dressing festival with medieval roots, Hartjesdag (Hearts Day) is like a block party for the Zeedijk, on the third weekend of August. Highly festive, and not just a gay scene.

Uitmarkt

www.uitmarkt.nl, in Dutch

All of Amsterdam's cultural venues preview their upcoming seasons at this mega arts event, which is complemented by a couple of big concerts on the last weekend in August. Outdoor stages are set up in the Eastern Docklands.

SEPTEMBER

Jordaan Festival

www.jordaanfestival.nl, in Dutch

Practitioners of the nostalgic, tears-in-your-beer music called *levenslied* – a speciality of the tight-knit Jordaan – take the stage in this late-September weekend event.

AT THE MOVIES

In July, and even more so in August, Amsterdam goes crazy for outdoor films. The major options:

> **Pluk de Nacht** (www.plukdenacht .nl) Two-week festival of international film, with screenings on the IJ.

> **Filmmuseum** (p103) Classics outdoors in Vondelpark during July and August.

> **Filmhuis Cavia** (www.filmhuis cavia.nl, in Dutch) Seventies classics and other must-sees at a different public space each Saturday in August.

> **Rialto** (www.rialtofilm.nl, in Dutch) At the Marie Heinekenplein in De Pijp for one weekend in late August.

Theaterfestival van Nederland en Vlaanderen

www.tf.nl

During the first two weeks of the month, this drama fest takes over most venues in the city, with a number of productions either in English or accompanied by projected translation. There's also the parallel Amsterdam Fringe Festival.

Amsterdam Design

www.amsterdamdesign.info

The whole month is dedicated to tours, talks and special exhibits highlighting ingenious Dutch design.

OCTOBER

Amsterdam Dance Event

www.amsterdam-dance-event.nl

A club music powwow, with 700 DJs and more than 40,000 avid dancers attending parties all over the city – all on one sweaty weekend late in the month.

ING Amsterdam Marathon

www.ingamsterdammarathon.nl

Some 25,000 runners race around the Rijksmuseum, Vondelpark and other city landmarks – an inspiring route for runners and an inspiring effort for spectators.

Robodock

www.robodock.org, in Dutch

If it's industrial, recycled and gives off lots of sparks and smoke, it's at Robodock, a long-running rough-and-tumble arts festival with its roots in the squat scene.

NOVEMBER

Museumnacht

www.n8.nl, in Dutch

For one night in late November, exhibition halls all over the city keep their doors open till 2am and schedule special performances, activities and parties. It's a good idea to buy tickets ahead – see the website for details.

International Documentary Film Festival

www.idfa.nl

Ten days in late November are dedicated to screening fascinating true stories from all over the world.

Sinterklaas Intocht

www.sintinamsterdam.nl, in Dutch

Marking the beginning of the holiday season in mid-November, Sinterklaas arrives by boat in the harbour and parades through town on his horse, tossing candy and ginger cookies to the city's entire child population. The date shifts each year, with festivities held all weekend.

DECEMBER

Oudejaarsavond

Fireworks-safety posters plaster the city in the month leading up to New Year's Eve, but they're no deterrent: at midnight, Amsterdam explodes with pyrotechnics – try to secure a spot indoors with a view.

CONCERT-GEBOUW

Robeco
Zomerconcerten

Robeco
Zomerconcerten

juli
augustus
2007

www.robecozomerconcerten.nl

Cool all summer

Locals enjoy a kick outside the Concertgebouw (p102)

ITINERARIES

Amsterdam is compact, so no need to focus on one neighbourhood a day – you can hopscotch all over with ease. As walking across the central canal ring takes less than an hour, you can squeeze a lot in, but to get the most out of your time, rent a bicycle (p175).

ONE DAY

Do your duty to art first: spin through the Rijksmuseum (p98) or Van Gogh Museum (p98) before the crowds arrive, then lunch by snacking your way along the Albert Cuypmarkt (p106) or having a late Turkish breakfast at Bazar (p109). Get yourself oriented by strolling the canal ring and browsing the Negen Straatjes (p14). At twilight, venture through De Wallen (the red-light district; p12), and have a drink at In de Olofspoort (p54) or 't Mandje (p56). Then do elegant Dutch at Greetje (p128) or Hemelse Modder (p128).

FORWARD PLANNING

Six months before you go Book your hotel, especially if you'll be visiting in the summer – top choices fill up very fast. (See p148 for some suggestions.)

Two to three months before you go Check the calendars for the Concertgebouw (p102), Muziekgebouw aan 't IJ (p139), Melkweg (p93) and Paradiso (p94) and buy tickets for anything that looks appealing.

Two weeks before you go Make reservations for De Kas (p117) or Bordewijk (p68). Book a massage at Deco Sauna (p77). Check programs of festivals (p22) and arrange a home dinner through www.like-a-local.com. Subscribe to the weekly bulletin at www.lecool.com. Take a brush-up spin on a bicycle, and attune your ears to the sound of a bike bell.

A few days before you go Make reservations at your top dinner choice for your first night in town (and your second, if you're organised enough). Buy tickets to the Rijksmuseum (p98), Van Gogh Museum (p98) and Anne Frank Huis (p62) online. Print out cycling tours of the Eastern Docklands (p132) from www.easterndocklands.com, download an audio tram tour (p138) or arrange a walk with Mee in Mokum (p178). Check the latest issue of *Amsterdam Weekly* at www.amsterdamweekly.com for event listings.

Top left See or be seen in Vondelpark (p18) **Top right** Here's looking at you: an example of Amsterdam's wacky street art **Bottom** De Kaaskamer cheese shop (p69) is heaven for cheese-lovers 't Smalle (p76) lies in the heart of the Jordaan and is unrivalled for *gezelligheid*

THREE DAYS

Follow the one-day itinerary, making time to sign up for a tour with the St Nicolaas Boat Club (p178) for your second day. On your second morning, visit the Anne Frank Huis (p62), lunch at Spanjer en van Twist (p72), then hop on your boat tour. Call in at the Uitburo (p93) for concert or show tickets, or hit the bars and clubs around the Leidseplein; De Zotte (p74) is a good place for a beer and simple meal beforehand. On day three, start the morning at Gartine (p48), then pop back over to De Wallen to see the Oude Kerk (p43). Lunch at grand cafe De Jaren (p47), and check out the scene at Vondelpark (p99). Have a casual dinner in the Jordaan at Festina Lente (p70), then enjoy a beer or two at 't Smalle (p76) or De Kat in de Wijngaert (p73).

WET WEATHER

Imagine yourself in sunnier climes at the Tropenmuseum (p113), then – if it's winter – go ice skating at Museumplein (p96). Visit Deco Sauna (p77) to warm up again, and keep the glow going with a hearty Dutch meal at Moeders (p70) or rib-sticking fondue at Café Bern (p127). Get your fix of *gezelligheid*, the cosy Dutch atmosphere that flourishes under grey skies, at any number of 'brown cafes' (p160). A *kopstot* (a shot of Dutch-style gin with a side of beer) works wonders. Then dance the night away at Paradiso (p94) or Melkweg (p93).

OFFBEAT AMSTERDAM

Visit specialised collections like the Bijbels Museum (p62) or the Tasen-museum Hendrikje (p85), and see Ons' Lieve Heer op Solder (p42), a church hidden in an attic. Continue the theme with Dutch-style pancakes at tiny Pannenkoekenhuis Upstairs (p51). Chill out with a joint and peruse the thrift goods at Sanementereng (p75), or head to De Looier (p65) for even more junk-cum-antiques. Submit to the chef's whims at a set-menu restaurant such as Gare de l'Est (p137) or Balthazar's Keuken (p68), or eat at squat restaurant De Peper (p101). Finally, check out whatever's on in the performance space at OT301 (p103).

FUN FOR FREE

Pop into the Begijnhof (p40), a hidden courtyard, and stroll through the Amsterdams Historisch Museum's Civic Guard Gallery (p40) to get your Golden Age fix (also admire the David and Goliath figures in the museum cafe). Attend a midday concert at the Concertgebouw (p102), learn all about the city's contemporary architecture at the Zuiderkerk (p125) and ARCAM (p133), then take in the view from the top of the Openbare Bibliotheek Amsterdam (public library; p136). People-watch at Vondelpark (p99), and join the Friday Night Skate (p99) from here, for an in-line tour through the city.

If you find a free table at De Jaren (p47), grab it quick!

NEIGHBOURHOODS

Amsterdam is a city that rewards aimless wandering. Narrow alleys contain random art installations. Views shift as you mount canal bridges. And the Dutch custom of curtainless windows seems designed to entertain flâneurs (and voyeurs).

That's good, because you'll almost certainly get lost. There's never a straight line in this town, just a zigzag of short streets and curving canals. The Centrum (the city centre) contains De Wallen (the red-light district), a bizarre juxtaposition of the modern sex industry with picturesque centuries-old buildings. In the Centrum's newer half, the city's intellectual life converges around the Spui, a square flanked by cafes and bookshops.

The Western Canal Belt is where dedicated shoppers spend their days, hopping from odd boutique to waterside cafe. To the west of here, the Jordaan is Amsterdam's Greenwich Village, a gentrified bohemia that is one of the best places in the city to get lost.

The canal ring completes its half-loop south of the centre. By day, visit the Southern Canal Belt's obscure museums; by night, party at the clubs around the area's two main squares. Just beyond the canals, Vondelpark is a green lung with personality, adjacent to the Old South, a genteel, quiet area that is a fitting home for the city's grandest museums. Next door, ethnic meets trendy in De Pijp, a neighbourhood where eateries serve cuisine from the Netherlands' former colonies.

Amsterdam's east side begins at the Nieuwmarkt and extends into the leafy expanse of the Plantage, the greenest area in this verdant city. Come here to browse the Waterlooplein flea market or to see the traces of Amsterdam's Jewish heritage. The highlight of the multiethnic Ooster-park district, just beyond, is the excellent Tropenmuseum.

In Amsterdam's harbour, the ever-changing skyline includes a state-of-the-art concert hall and extends into the edgy Eastern Docklands, adored by the design clique for its architectural experimentation.

>CITY CENTRE

The medieval core of Amsterdam is split down the middle by the Damrak. To the east lies the Oude Zijde (Old Side), with De Wallen (the red-light district) at its northern end. Far from being a no-go area, it has some beautiful historical bars, as well as the stunning Oude Kerk (p43), the city's oldest church. The Zeedijk, on the northeast side, marks the location of the city's old sea wall. Since the late 19th century, it has been Amsterdam's Chinatown, but it's also a symbol of urban rebirth: in the 1980s, the street was a major junkie hangout, but it's now home to a Buddhist temple, tiny boutiques and some excellent bars. South of the Dam, the skinny Nes was once a long row of monasteries; now it's the theatre district. At the southern end of the Oude Zijde, the University of Amsterdam (UvA) occupies a cluster of grand old buildings.

West of the Damrak, the Nieuwe Zijde (New Side), is only a century or so younger, but it does feel noticeably more modern. Trams run along filled-in canals, and the city's main mass-market shopping streets, Nieuwendijk and Kalverstraat, are a swath of chain shops. But in the tiny alleys connecting the main avenues, which are barely wide enough for two people to pass, you'll find surprising bars and cafes. The Spui, a plaza near the south end of the area, is an intellectual hub for the city – there's more UvA campus over here, several excellent bookshops and a weekly book market. The numerous casual cafe-bars in the area cater both to students and after-work beer-drinkers.

The Damrak, one of the city centre's busiest thoroughfares

CITY CENTRE

🔵 SEE

Amsterdams
  Historisch Museum 1   B7
Begijnhof 2   B7
Beurs van Berlage 3   D4
Civic Guard Gallery 4   B7
Dam Square & Nationaal
  Monument 5   C5
Guan Yin Shrine 6   E5
Hash, Marihuana
  & Hemp Museum 7   D6
Koninklijk Paleis 8   B5
Nieuwe Kerk 9   B5
Ons' Lieve Heer
  op Solder 10   D4
Oude Kerk 11   D5
Prostitution
  Information Centre 12   D4
Schreierstoren 13   E3
Sexmuseum
  Amsterdam 14   D3

🔲 SHOP

Athenaeum 15   A7
Condomerie 16   C5
Conscious Dreams
  Kokopelli 17   D4
De Bijenkorf 18   C5
Female & Partners 19   B4
Fred de la Bretonière 20   B6
Geels & Co. 21   D4
Hans Appenzeller 22   C7
HEMA 23   B8
HEMA 24   C4

Jacob Hooy & Co 25   E6
Laundry Industry 26   B7
Laundry Industry 27   B5
Maison de Bonneterie .. 28   B8
Open 29   B6
Oudemanhuispoort
  Book Market 30   C7
Outland Records 31   E4
PGC Hajenius 32   B7
Rush Hour Records 33   B4
Sissy-Boy 34   B5
Wonderwood 35   D7

🍴 EAT

De Bakkerswinkel 36   D4
De Jaren 37   C8
De Keuken van
  1870 38   C3
Dop 39   B7
Dwaze Zaken 40   E3
Gartine 41   B7
Hofje van Wijs 42   E4
Kam Yin 43   D3
Kapitein Zeppo's 44   C7
La Place 45   C8
Lanskroon 46   A7
Lucius 47   A6
Nam Kee 48   E5
New King 49   E5
Pannenkoekenhuis
  Upstairs 50   C7
Rob Wigboldus
  Vishandel 51   C5
'Skek 52   E3
Supperclub 53   B6

Thais Snackbar
  Bird 54   E4
Van Kerkwijk 55   C6
Villa Zeezicht 56   B4
Vlaams Frites
  Huis 57   B8

🍸 DRINK

Abraxas 58   B6
Crea 59   C7
Dampkring 60   B8
Diep 61   B6
Getto 62   D4
Gollem 63   A7
Greenhouse 64   D6
Het Schuim 65   A6
Hoppe 66   A7
In 't Aepjen 67   E3
In de Olofspoort 68   E3
Kadinsky 69   B7
Latei 70   E5
Lime 71   E5
't Mandje 72   E4
Van Zuylen 73   B4
Vrankrijk 74   A6
Wijnand Fockink 75   C6

⭐ PLAY

Bitterzoet 76   C3
Casa Rosso 77   D5
Casablanca 78   E4
Winston Kingdom 79   D5

Please see over for map

NEIGHBOURHOODS

CITY CENTRE

☉ SEE

☉ AMSTERDAMS HISTORISCH MUSEUM

☎ 523 18 22; www.ahm.nl; Nieuwezijds Voorburgwal 357; admission €6/3;
⏱ 10am-5pm Mon-Fri, 11am-5pm Sat &
Sun; 🚊 1/2/5 Spui; ♿

You won't find any dusty relics here – the city's history museum covers the early years well, but just as interesting are the exhibits on the past century. You can peek into typical Amsterdam apartments, hear immigrants' stories and even visit a recreation of 't Mandje (p56), the historic gay bar. Don't miss the **Civic Guard Gallery** (free entrance) in the alley on the southern side of the museum, which is lined with grand posed group portraits from the Dutch Golden Age.

☉ BEGIJNHOF

☎ 622 19 18; www.begijnhofamster
dam.nl; Spui, north side; ⏱ 8am-5pm;
🚊 1/2/5 Spui; ♿

This quiet courtyard and the houses around it were built for the Beguines, a lay Catholic sisterhood. After the Protestant Alteration in 1578, the women worshipped in a chapel hidden in a house. It is decorated with paintings depicting the Miracle of Amsterdam (boxed text, opposite). English Puritans took over the church in the yard; look for pulpit panels by Piet Mondrian, in a figurative phase. The last of the sisters died in 1971, but the houses here are still reserved for women. In the hallway from the Spui, look for carvings of dogs, chickens and men – all things prohibited here, in order to keep the peace.

Mingle with the pigeons on the Dam

MMM, TASTY – & MIRACULOUS!

In 1345 a dying man received the final sacrament, but he later vomited up the Host (communion wafer). His nurse tossed the mess in the fire, but the Host would not burn – and the man was shortly restored to health. Once word got out about the miraculous flame-retardant wafer and its healing powers, pilgrims flocked to Amsterdam; even future Hapsburg emperor Maximilian came to be healed in the 15th century. Paintings and a mural depicting the Miracle of Amsterdam hang in the chapel in the Begijnhof (opposite), and every year on 12 March, the Stille Omgang (Silent Procession) along the Heiligeweg honours the event, with thousands of people attending.

⊙ BEURS VAN BERLAGE

www.bvb.nl; Damrak 277; ⌚ **10am-6pm Mon-Sat, 11am-6pm Sun;** 🚊 **4/9/16/24/25 Dam**

Master architect and ardent socialist HP Berlage (1856–1934) built this financial exchange in 1903. He filled the temple of capitalism with decorations that venerate labour – look inside the cafe to see tile murals of the well-muscled proletariat of the past, present and future. The present bourse is located across the street, and this building now contains concert halls and expo space; tours are available by appointment through Artifex (p178).

⊙ DAM SQUARE & NATIONAAL MONUMENT

Dam Square; 🚊 **4/9/16/24/25 Dam**

This pigeon-filled expanse was the site of the original dam built across the Amstel. Now it's busker central, with the occasional puppet show during summer and a Ferris wheel in the spring. The obelisk on the east side is the Nationaal Monument, built in 1956 to honour the fallen of WWII.

⊙ GUAN YIN SHRINE

Fo Guang Shan He Hua Temple; ☎ **420 23 57; www.ibps.nl; Zeedijk 106-118;** ⌚ **noon-5pm Tue-Sat (also Mon Jun-Sep), 10am-5pm Sun;** 🚊 **4/9/16/24/25 Dam**

Queen Beatrix presided over the opening of this Buddhist temple, the first in the Netherlands, in 2000. The ornate 'mountain gate' brings a bit of high-altitude Asia to these lowlands, though the interior is relatively small and spare. Recitations of the sutras (sayings of the Buddha) are held every Sunday at 10.30am.

HASH, MARIHUANA & HEMP MUSEUM

☎ 623 59 61; Oudezijds Achterburgwal 148; admission €5.70; ⏲ 11am-10pm; 🚊 4/9/16/24/25 Dam

A helter-skelter review of marijuana trivia, this place has a few interesting tidbits, but basically exists as a showcase for its impressive grow room – conveniently adjacent to a seed shop.

KONINKLIJK PALEIS

☎ 620 40 60; www.koninklijkhuis.nl; Dam Square; 🚊 1/2/5/13/14/17 Raadhuisstraat; ♿

Commissioned as a town hall in 1648, this building became a royal palace in the 19th century. Even when the place isn't being renovated (the estimated reopening is spring 2009), Queen Beatrix lives in Den Haag and only uses this for ceremonies. Its sombre facade belies an interior of gold and marble.

NIEUWE KERK

☎ 638 69 09; www.nieuwekerk.nl; Dam Square; admission €4; ⏲ 10am-6pm; 🚊 1/2/5/13/14/17 Raadhuisstraat; ♿

When not hosting coronations and royal weddings, the New Church (dating from 1408 – it's all relative) exhibits treasures from other cultures and countries. Check out the cool modern stained glass, the 10m-tall pulpit and the monuments to the Netherlands' great maritime heroes.

ONS' LIEVE HEER OP SOLDER

Museum Amstelkring; ☎ 624 66 04; www.museumamstelkring.nl; Oudezijds Voorburgwal 40; admission €7/5; ⏲ 10am-5pm Mon-Sat, 1-5pm Sun; 🚊 4/9/16/24/25 Centraal Station

Built in 1661 during the Calvinist era, Our Lord in the Attic was a Catholic church hidden on the

OLD AMSTERDAM MEETS NEW

In the spring of 1609, explorer Henry Hudson sailed his ship *De Halve Maan* (The Half Moon) from Amsterdam's harbour and off to the New World, where he found the ideal spot for a trading post. This became New Amsterdam, capital of New Netherland. Four hundred years (and a treaty with the British) later, it's better known as New York, but historians argue that the early Amsterdam expats are responsible for making the city what it is today: a multiethnic, business-first metropolis. Just like Amsterdam, but bigger – and without so many bicycles. You can read all about it in Russell Shorto's excellent history *The Island at the Centre of the World*.

upper floors of a canal house. A tour of the whole house, via labyrinthine staircases, passes through simple living spaces, a snug 'between room' and into the soaring, two-storey church, complete with organ. From outside, it's difficult to see how everything fits into the skinny building.

◎ OUDE KERK
☎ 625 82 84; www.oudekerk.nl; Oudekerksplein 23; admission €5/4; ☽ 11am-5pm Mon-Sat, 1-5pm Sun; ⊟ 4/9/16/24/25 Dam; ♿

The city's oldest building and earliest parish church was established in 1200, though the original wooden structure was replaced with stone around 1300. The most remarkable element is the ceiling: some of the dark wood boards date from 1480, and images of saints still glow faintly. Sunday services are held at 11am, but the church is largely used for exhibitions, most notably the World Press Photo exhibit every April (p22). Outside, look in the cobblestones for a bronze panel of a breast – a bit of guerrilla art installed anonymously.

◎ PROSTITUTION INFORMATION CENTRE
☎ 420 73 28; www.pic-amsterdam.com; Enge Kerksteeg 3; ☽ noon-7pm Tue-Sat; ⊟ 4/9/16/24/25 Dam

Burning questions about the red-light district? Head here for answers, provided by current and former sex workers. At press time, the centre was undergoing a redesign – it will soon have some exhibits on prostitution in addition to books on the subject. Better though, is the excellent **walking tour** (5pm Sat; €12.50), which takes you into a working room.

◎ SCHREIERSTOREN
☎ 428 82 91; Prins Hendrikkade 94-95; ⊟ 4/9/16/24/25 Centraal Station

Built around 1480 as part of the city's defences, this brick tower became a point from which women waved farewell to ships. Inside, in the nautical-theme VOC Café, look for a 1569 stone plaque depicting such a woman – she's probably weeping because, in those days, only one in three sailors ever returned safely from a sea journey. Outside, a plaque commemorates Henry Hudson's sailing from here (see the boxed text, opposite).

◎ SEXMUSEUM AMSTERDAM
☎ 622 83 76; www.sexmuseumamsterdam.nl; Damrak 18; admission €3; ☽ 10am-11.30pm; ⊟ 1/2/5/13/17 Centraal Station

A temple to titillation through the ages that provides more sniggers than serious contemplation. Animatronics have never been put to such odd use – and what is that woman doing with that squid? Visitors must be 16 years old and over.

🛍 SHOP

🏠 ATHENAEUM *Books*
☎ 514 14 60; Spui 14-16; 🚊 1/2/5 Spui
Amsterdam's savviest bookshop is a bit of an intellectual and style hub. Its adjoining newsagency has cutting-edge international magazines, newspapers and guidebooks.

🏠 CONDOMERIE *Sex Shop*
☎ 627 41 74; Warmoesstraat 141; 🕐 Mon-Sat; 🚊 4/9/16/24/25 Dam
Putting the 'pro' back in prophylactic: rarely can you shop for a condom in such a tasteful setting, with such a fabulous (borderline mind-boggling) selection. Grab a mixed trial pack if you can't decide.

🏠 CONSCIOUS DREAMS KOKOPELLI *Smart Shop*
☎ 421 70 00; Warmoesstraat 12; 🕐 11am-10pm; 🚊 4/9/16/24/25 Centraal Station
A branch of the city's oldest and most reputable smart shop (p86).

🏠 DE BIJENKORF *Department Store*
☎ 621 80 80; www.bijenkorf .nl, in Dutch; Dam 1; 🕐 11am-7pm Mon, 9.30am-7pm Tue, Wed & Sat, 9.30am-9pm Thu & Fri, noon-6pm Sun; 🚊 4/9/16/24/25 Dam
The prestigious 'Beehive', established in 1850 and now housed in a 1957 Marcel Breuer block, is indeed a busy place, its five floors full of shoppers picking through designer brands from home (G-Star Raw Denim, for instance) and abroad (DKNY, etc). The top-floor cafe has a great view.

QUICK(IE) FACTS
In De Wallen (the red-light district), prostitution is an industry like any other. You'll see specialisation – an NL sticker in a window, indicating 'Dutch spoken here', and sections occupied by Surinamese-, Russian- or Spanish-speaking women – and of course aggressive self-marketing. Women pay between €75 and €150 to rent a window for an eight- or 10-hour shift (the rate depends on the facilities, but all rooms have a bed and a sink), and charge between €35 and €50 for a blowjob or a quickie (15 minutes or less). They also pay income taxes based on city estimates of income correlated with tourism figures. No wonder – allegedly some 40% of the customers are British.

In Amsterdam, fun comes in all shapes and sizes

FEMALE & PARTNERS
Sex Shop
☎ 620 91 52; Spuistraat 100; ⏲ 1-6pm Sun & Mon, 11am-6pm Tue-Sat, 11am-9pm Thu; 🚊 1/2/5/13/14/17 Raadhuisstraat

The sign on the door says 'Push (harder)', setting the tone for this sex-toy shop that doesn't take itself too seriously. It stocks nontrashy lingerie and body jewellery designed by the female owners, along with vibrators, toys and DVDs.

FRED DE LA BRETONIÈRE
Footwear
☎ 623 41 52; Sint Luciënsteeg 20; 🚊 1/2/5/14 Paleisstraat

This Dutch shoe designer's products are solid and not terribly expensive, as if made to ride a bicycle in. That sounds dull, but in fact Fred satisfies the burning need for both a sensible heel and a knee-high boot in candy-apple red leather. Men's shoes are also available, though the colour spectrum isn't as broad.

GEELS & CO *Food & Drink*
☎ 624 06 83; Warmoesstraat 67; ⏲ 9.30am-6pm Mon-Sat; 🚊 4/9/16/24/25 Dam

The distinguished Geels & Co has been roasting coffees and selling loose-leaf tea for 140 years. Not only does it smell great, but there are charming teapots, coffee pots and brewing paraphernalia for sale.

HANS APPENZELLER
Jewellery
☎ 626 82 18; Grimburgwal 1; ⏲ Tue-Sat; 🚊 4/9/14/16/24/25 Spui

Appenzeller is one of Amsterdam's leading designers in gold and stone. If his spare work is not your style, check out the other jewellers along the street.

HEMA *Clothing, Housewares*
☎ 623 41 76; Nieuwendijk 174; ⏲ 10.30am-6.30pm Mon, 9.30am-6.30pm Tue, Wed, Fri & Sat, 9.30am-9pm Thu, noon-6pm Sun; 🚊 4/9/16/24/25 Dam

Check the label on any Dutch behind: HEMA, a Dutch five-and-dime that's as fun as it is functional, is the place to go for underwear…plus kitchen towels, espresso cups and bike accessories. There's another branch at the **Kalvertoren shopping centre** (Kalverstraat 212).

🏠 JACOB HOOY & CO
Perfume & Cosmetics
☎ 624 30 41; Kloveniersburgwal 12; 🕐 Mon-Sat; 🚋 4/9/16/24/25 Dam
This chemist's shop has been selling medicinal herbs, homeopathic remedies and natural cosmetics since 1743, and its interior, lined with wooden drawers, has barely changed.

🏠 LAUNDRY INDUSTRY
Clothing
☎ 420 25 54; Spui 1; 🚋 4/9/14/16/24/25 Spui
This cool Dutch label specialises in minimalist functional fashion in neutrals, but with attractive details like pintucking and shirring. There's another in **Magna Plaza** (Spuistraat 137).

🏠 MAISON DE BONNETERIE
Department Store
☎ 531 34 00; Rokin 140; 🚋 4/9/14/16/24/25 Muntplein
Amsterdam's establishment, including Queen Beatrix, likes to shop at this grand old department store. A bit flashier and more exclusive than De Bijenkorf (p44).

🏠 OPEN
Clothing
☎ 528 69 63; Nieuwzijds Voorburgwal 291; 🕐 noon-7pm, noon-9pm Thu; 🚋 1/2/5/14 Paleisstraat
This tiny shop showcases 10 different designers – a bit of repurposed vintage chic, a bit of creative knit jersey, and some tongue-in-cheek Dutch milkmaid skirts. We like 100% Halal, a line of East-meets-West street style.

🏠 OUDEMANHUIS BOOK MARKET
Books
Oudemanhuispoort; 🕐 11am-4pm Mon-Fri; 🚋 4/9/14/16/24/25 Spui
A favourite with academics, this moody old covered alleyway connecting two streets is lined with second-hand booksellers. Most of the material is in Dutch, but one vendor specialises in cookbooks, many in English.

🏠 OUTLAND RECORDS
Music
☎ 638 75 76; Zeedijk 22; 🕐 11am-7pm Mon-Sat, 11am-9pm Thu, noon-6pm Sun; 🚋 4/9/16/24/25 Centraal Station
A purist's club-music shop with vinyl only, plus designer Japanese toys and rhinestone-encrusted headphones. Get info and tickets for parties here.

🏠 PGC HAJENIUS
Speciality Shop
☎ 623 74 94; Rokin 96; 🚋 4/9/14/16/24/25 Spui

Even if you're not a cigar connoisseur, stroll through this tobacco emporium for a glimpse of the grandeur that used to line the Rokin in the early 20th century. Inside is all art deco stained glass, gilt trim and soaring ceilings. Regular customers, including members of the Dutch royal family, have private humidors here.

🎧 RUSH HOUR RECORDS
Music
☎ 427 45 05; Spuistraat 98; ⏱ 1-7pm Mon, 11am-7pm Tue-Sat, 11am-9pm Thu, 1-6pm Sun; 🚊 1/2/5/13/14/17 Raadhuisstraat

This club-music record shop is a bit of a hangout for local DJs and a good source for party info and tickets. The bargain used-vinyl bins often have some old-school gems.

🎧 SISSY-BOY
Clothing, Housewares
☎ 389 25 89; Spuistraat 137; ⏱ 11am-7pm Mon, 10am-7pm Tue-Sat, to 9pm Thu, noon-7pm Sun; 🚊 1/2/5/13/14/17 Raadhuisstraat

Never mind the name – this Dutch clothing chain sells quirky print shirts and other items that tread the line between preppie and hip. This large branch in the basement of the Magna Plaza shopping centre also stocks lots of home items.

🎧 WONDERWOOD *Design*
☎ 625 37 38; Rusland 3; ⏱ noon-6pm Wed-Sat; 🚊 4/9/14/16/24/25 Spui

As much a museum as a shop, here you can ogle the sensuous, delicate moulded-plywood creations of George Nelson, Marcel Breuer and more – some of the vintage pieces are for sale, and some available in reissue. If that's impractical, smaller art objects (made of wood, naturally) are also available.

🍴 EAT

🍴 DE BAKKERSWINKEL
Cafe & Bakery   €
☎ 489 80 00; Warmoesstraat 69; ⏱ 8am-6pm Tue-Fri, 8am-5pm Sat, 10am-5pm Sun; 🚊 4/9/16/24/25 Dam; Ⓥ ♿

Right on the hot-and-heavy Warmoesstraat is this family-friendly cafe with excellent baked goods, especially scones. There's a kids' play area out back.

🍴 DE JAREN *Cafe*   €
☎ 625 57 71; Nieuwe Doelenstraat 20-22; ⏱ 10am-1am; 🚊 4/9/14/16/24/25 Muntplein; Ⓥ ♿

This big, buzzy and bright bar-cafe-restaurant is one of the city's best, thanks in part to its handy location and two large terraces on the water. It's the kind of place where you head for a coffee and

NEIGHBOURHOODS

CITY CENTRE

end up leaving hours later having consumed an entire magazine, a satisfying sandwich and a glass or two of wine.

🍴 DE KEUKEN VAN 1870
Dutch   €

☎ 620 40 18; Spuistraat 4; ⏱ lunch & dinner Mon-Sat; 🚊 1/2/5/13/17 Martelaarsgracht; Ⓥ ♿

Though it's white and airy inside, rather than wood-panelled, this bargain restaurant is as Dutch as it comes. The three-course set menu (€8.50) involves *stamppot* (mashed veg and potatoes) and *vla* (pudding). Bachelors read newspapers and sip glasses of milk. A cat roams around. And the service is surly – just consider that a cultural experience.

🍴 DOP *Sandwich Shop*   €

☎ 624 75 51; Taksteeg 7; ⏱ 10.30am-5.30pm Mon, 10am-5.30pm Tue-Fri, 10am-6pm Thu, 11am-7pm Sat; 🚊 4/9/14/16/24/25 Spui

Sandwiches at Dop may look simple, but they're certainly not skimpy – your white roll comes slathered with plenty of butter and an ample portion of, for example, leg of lamb, roast beef or liverwurst. With a side of *frites* (that, dare we say, beat those at Vlaams Frites Huis, p53), you have a real workhorse Dutch lunch.

🍴 DWAZE ZAKEN *Cafe*   €

☎ 612 41 75; Prins Hendrikkade 50; ⏱ noon-midnight Mon-Sat, kitchen to 9pm; 🚊 4/9/16/24/25 Centraal Station; Ⓥ ♿

A refuge from red-light madness, this mosaic-trimmed corner cafe has big windows and a menu of spicy wraps and creative fondue. Wash it down with a good selection of beer, and stay for live jazz on Thursdays. The bathrooms are by far the nicest in the Centrum.

🍴 GARTINE *Cafe*   €

☎ 320 41 32; Taksteeg 7; ⏱ 8am-6pm Wed-Sun; 🚊 4/9/14/16/24/25 Spui; Ⓥ

Gartine makes delectable breakfast pastries, sandwiches and salads from produce grown in its own garden plot. Throw in slow-food credentials and gorgeous antique plates and it's a winner, and a rare bright spot in the dull Kalverstraat area.

🍴 HOFJE VAN WIJS *Cafe*   €

☎ 624 04 36; Zeedijk 43; ⏱ noon-6pm Tue & Wed, 10am-10.30pm Thu, 9am-10.30pm Fri & Sat, 10am-7pm Sun; 🚊 4/9/16/24/25 Centraal Station

The 200-year-old coffee and tea vendor Wijs & Zonen maintains this pretty courtyard cafe. In addition to the usual offerings (tasty cakes!), it serves inexpensive couscous and pasta dinners. The place even runs a weekly **walking**

Berna Meijer

Tour guide at the Prostitution Information Centre (p43)

Loving her job No question is taboo. Like, I asked a prostitute, 'What's "the turtle"'? She said, 'Get on the floor…'. **Relax** It's OK to look. But there's a difference between looking and staring – you're not at a zoo. Give a smile – they're normal women, and they appreciate it. **Don't miss…** Look at the crooked buildings, and details like the boobie by the Oude Kerk (p43). **Best time** In the summer, when it's just getting dark – you really taste the bubbly vibe. **Best eats** Kam Yin (p50) is very cheap and has the best roti. **Best bar** Casablanca (p57)! It's great for karaoke, but don't go if you're claustrophobic. **A quieter drink** In de Olofspoort (p54) has old-fashioned liqueurs with weird names, like the 'missy in green'. **Best sex show** Casa Rosso (p57) really tries to make women feel comfortable.

tour (3pm Sun), which begins with coffee and *appeltaart*.

🍴 KAM YIN *Surinamese* €
☎ 625 31 15; Warmoesstraat 8; 🕐 noon-midnight; 🚊 4/9/16/24/25 Centraal Station; Ⓥ ♿

It's nothing much to look at, but this plastic and fluorescent operation nonetheless dispenses excellent versions of Surinamese standards like roti and *tjauw min* (thick noodles with assorted meats). Its *broodje pom* (a chicken-casserole sandwich) rivals De Tokoman's (p128).

🍴 KAPITEIN ZEPPO'S
Cafe €€
☎ 624 20 57; Gebed Zonder End 5; 🕐 lunch & dinner; 🚊 4/9/14/16/24/25 Spui; ♿

In an alley off Grimburgwal, this bar-cafe has a timeless bohemian feel, whether at the tiletop, candlelit tables or in the covered winter garden. There's a light brasserie menu, and the restaurant upstairs is also good, featuring Amsterdam's best waiters; a crew of older Italian men.

🍴 LA PLACE *Cafe* €
☎ 235 83 63; Kalverstraat 201; 🕐 10am-7pm Mon-Fri, 10am-9pm Sat, noon-6pm Sun; 🚊 4/9/14/16/24/25 Muntplein; ♿ Ⓥ ♿

On the 1st floor of the Vroom & Dreesmann department store,

this deluxe cafeteria has a little something for everyone: sandwiches, quiches, stir-fries, pastas, all freshly prepared. The ground-floor Le Marché has takeaway sandwiches.

🍴 LANSKROON
Bakery & Sweets €
☎ 623 74 43; Singel 385; 🕐 8am-5.30pm Mon-Fri, 9am-5.30pm Sat, 10am-5.30 Sun; 🚊 1/2/5 Spui; Ⓥ ♿

Other historic bakeries have prettier fixtures and daintier cakes, but only humble Lanskroon has such a remarkable *stroopwafel* – crispy, big as a dessert plate and available with caramel, honey or a deceptively healthy-tasting fig paste. In winter, locals come for spicy *speculaas* cookies and other holiday treats, and there's ice cream in the summer.

🍴 LUCIUS *Seafood* €€
☎ 624 18 31; Spuistraat 247; 🕐 5pm-midnight; 🚊 1/2/5 Spui

Delicious and consistently full, Lucius is known for simple but expertly prepared fish, such as Dover sole in butter and giant North Sea oysters. The interior, decked-out with fish tanks and tiles, is workmanlike and professional, just like the service. It's perhaps a little more expensive than it ought to be, but it's also a rare restaurant that's open so late.

🍴 NAM KEE Chinese €
☎ 624 34 70; Zeedijk 111-113; 🕑 noon-11pm; 🚃 4/9/16/24/25 Dam; 🅥

Venerable Nam Kee's steamed oysters with black-bean sauce are legendary in Amsterdam. They are delicious, but the atmosphere can be grim (and we have a high tolerance for fluorescent lights). A second location nearby (p129) is nicer.

🍴 NEW KING Chinese €€
☎ 625 21 80; Zeedijk 115-117; 🕑 11.30am-midnight; 🚃 4/9/16/24/25 Dam; 🅥

We *would* recommend this place over next-door neighbour Nam Kee (above) – great duck soup, garlicky greens and other Cantonese staples, plus superior atmosphere – but in fact the oysters really aren't as good. Maybe plan a two-stage meal.

🍴 PANNENKOEKENHUIS UPSTAIRS Dutch €
☎ 626 56 03; Grimburgwal 2; 🕑 noon-5pm; 🚃 4/9/14/16/24/25 Spui; 🅥 ♿

If you can make it up the steep stairs – then actually find a seat in this tiny place – you'll be able to savour some of the tastiest and least expensive pancakes in town. It's a one-man show, so service

operates at its own pace. One other hurdle: it might not always be open during posted hours.

🍴 ROB WIGBOLDUS VISHANDEL Sandwich Shop €
☎ 626 33 88; Zoutsteeg 6; 🕑 breakfast & lunch; 🚃 4/9/16/24/25 Dam

A wee oasis in the midst of surrounding tourist tat, this fish shop in a tiny alley serves excellent herring sandwiches (on a choice of crusty white or brown rolls, no less). Don't like fish? Van den Berg, right next door, does all the meaty *broodjes* (breadrolls).

🍴 'SKEK Cafe €
☎ 427 05 51; Zeedijk 4-8; noon-1am Sun-Thu, noon-3am Fri & Sat; 🚃 4/9/16/24/25 Centraal Station; ♿ 🅥 ♿

Run by students for students (flashing your ID gets you one-third off), this friendly, fun cafe-bar is a nice place to get some healthy food. Bands occasionally perform at night.

🍴 SUPPERCLUB International €€€
☎ 638 05 13; www.supperclub.nl; Jonge Roelensteeg 21; 🕑 8pm-1am Wed-Sat; 🚃 1/2/5/14 Paleisstraat; 🅥

Supperclub is an Amsterdam institution, but it changes every night. The only certainties are that you'll be served five courses of very

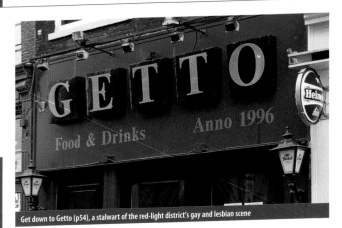

Get down to Getto (p54), a stalwart of the red-light district's gay and lesbian scene

high-concept food and people will be performing something around or with you. And you'll have to take your shoes off, as you'll be sprawled on a cushion while it happens. In good weather, take the Supperclub Cruise, on a boat out on the IJ.

🍴 THAIS SNACKBAR BIRD
Thai €
☎ 620 14 42; Zeedijk 77; ⏱ 2-10pm; 🚋 4/9/16/24/25 Centraal Station
Don't tell the Chinese neighbours, but this is some of the best Asian food on the Zeedijk – the cooks, wedged in a tiny kitchen, don't skimp on lemongrass, fish sauce or chilli. There's a bit more room to spread out in the (slightly pricier) restaurant across the street (No 72).

🍴 VAN KERKWIJK
International €€
☎ 620 33 16; Nes 41; ⏱ lunch & dinner; 🚋 4/9/16/24/25 Dam; Ⓥ ♿
Exceptionally warm service – your waitress may sit down and chat before reciting the menu – and interesting, reasonably priced food make this a personal-feeling spot in a somewhat generic part of the city. Although the creative combos don't always hit the mark, the ingredients are fresh and deftly prepared. We recommend the calamari, and the pear tart. Bonus: reservations aren't necessary.

🍴 VILLA ZEEZICHT *Cafe* €
☎ 626 74 33; Torensteeg 7; ⏱ 7.30am-9pm; 🚋 1/2/5/13/14/17 Raadhuisstraat; Ⓥ ♿

While Villa Zeezicht does some decent lunch items, it's all just clumsy foreplay for the home-made apple tart with cream that is a deserved Amsterdam legend.

🍴 VLAAMS FRITES HUIS
Fast Food €
☎ 624 60 75; Voetboogstraat 33; ⏰ 11am-6pm Tue-Sat, noon-6pm Sun & Mon; 🚊 1/2/5 Koningsplein; ♿ Ⓥ ♿

Long known as the best place for fried potatoes in Amsterdam, this hole-in-the-wall stand doles them out to *frites* devotees. The sauce selection is vast. (Don't fall for the similarly named place on *Hand*boogstraat.)

🍸 DRINK
🍸 ABRAXAS *Coffeeshop*
☎ 625 57 63; Jonge Roelensteeg 12; ⏰ 10am-1am; 🚊 1/2/5/14 Paleisstraat

The Abraxas management seems to know exactly what stoners want: mellow music, comfy sofas, rooms with different energy levels and, of course, thick milkshakes. The considerate staff and friendly, young clientele make this a fantastic place for coffeeshop newbies. The same owners run a much smaller space at Spuistraat 51.

🍸 CREA *Cafe*
☎ 525 14 23; Turfdraagsterpad 17; ⏰ 10am-1am Mon-Sat, 11am-7pm Sun; 🚊 4/9/14/16/24/25 Spui; Ⓥ ♿

Walking along Grimburgwal, you can't help but notice the prime cafe chairs across the canal. They're part of the University of Amsterdam's cultural centre, a laid-back spot with an excellent view of the bridge once known as *the* place to buy a stolen bike – you might still witness the occasional transaction.

🍸 DAMPKRING *Coffeeshop*
☎ 638 07 05; Handboogstraat 29; ⏰ 10am-1am Sun-Thu, 10pm-2am Sat & Sun; 🚊 1/2/5 Koningsplein

Most famous for its cameo in *Ocean's Twelve,* the moodily lit Dampkring also has a solid selection of weed and helpful staff. The company has expanded its special *dampkring* (atmosphere) to a nearby shop at Heisteeg 6 (signed as De Tweede Kamer, and sporting an excellent art deco interior), and another where Heisteeg meets Singel.

🍸 DIEP *Lounge*
☎ 420 20 20; Nieuwezijds Voorburgwal 256; ⏰ 5pm-1am Mon-Thu, 5pm-3am Fri & Sat; 🚊 1/2/5/14 Paleisstraat

The disco ball, chandeliers and chocolate interior at this otherwise laid-back bar give it a kitsch-camp feel. While it's low-key early in the evening, it gets crowded with cool young locals later on when the DJs do their thing.

⛄ GETTO *Gay & Lesbian*
☎ 421 51 51; Warmoesstraat 51; ⏲ Tue-Sun 5pm-1am; 🚊 4/9/16/24/25 Centraal Station

Getto is a haven for a younger gay and lesbian crowd and anyone who wants a little bohemian subculture in the middle of De Wallen (the red-light district). Its inclusive feel is aided by the two-for-one daily happy hour from 5pm to 7pm; food is good and cheap too.

⛄ GOLLEM *Beer Bar*
☎ 626 66 45; Raamsteeg 4; 🚊 1/2/5 Spui

All the brew-related paraphernalia in this miniscule space barely leaves room for the 200 beers – mostly from Belgium – and the connoisseurs who come to try them. The bartenders are happy to advise.

⛄ GREENHOUSE *Coffeeshop*
☎ 627 17 39; Oudezijds Voorburgwal 191; ⏲ 9am-1am Mon-Thu & Sun, 9am-3am Fri & Sat; 🚊 4/9/16/24/25 Dam

This branch of the original in De Pijp (p111) is decorated just as nicely, making it the classiest place in De Wallen. This one has no fiddly 'membership' business.

⛄ HET SCHUIM *Bar*
☎ 638 93 57; Spuistraat 189; ⏲ 11am-1am Mon-Thu, 11am-3am Fri & Sat, 1pm-1am Sun; 🚊 1/2/5/14 Paleisstraat

Schuim means 'foam' and this arty bar doles it out – on the tops of beers – at a rapid rate. There's usually a substantial crowd here, but the place is relatively spacious and there are tables outside and big windows, so you can take a seat and watch artists, professionals and general street oddities mingle.

⛄ HOPPE *Brown Cafe*
☎ 420 44 20; Spui 18; ⏲ 8am-1am Mon-Thu, 8am-2am Fri & Sat; 🚊 1/2/5 Spui

Boasting the city's highest beer turnover, this busy spot has been in business since 1670. Its cosy interior, with recycled church pews and beer barrels, tends to attract more camera-wielding tourists than locals, but a side entrance on Heisteeg leads to a smaller, quieter room dedicated to *jenever* (Dutch-style gin).

⛄ IN DE OLOFSPOORT *Tasting House*
☎ 624 39 18; Nieuwbrugsteeg 13; ⏲ 4pm-midnight Tue & Thu-Sat; 🚊 4/9/16/24/25 Centraal Station

Head here for more heady liqueurs after Wijnand Fockink (p56) shuts. A crew of regulars has dedicated bottles stocked just for them.

NO SMOKING (MOSTLY)

Following the trend in other European and American cities, Amsterdam banned smoking in all bars and restaurants on 1 July 2008, while this book was being researched. A particularly devoted lot, Dutch smokers nonetheless stowed their packets of Drum tobacco and admitted it's probably for the best. But coffeeshops remain: smoking marijuana is legit – but for a cigarette, sorry, you'll have to step outside. Some bigger coffeeshops have installed special 'self-service' (no employees allowed) rooms where you can still enjoy a standard euro-style tobacco-laced joint. Smaller places have stocked up on bongs and vaporisers and posted signs saying 'Pure marijuana only!' Only in Amsterdam, kids, only in Amsterdam.

▼ IN 'T AEPJEN *Brown Cafe*
☎ 626 84 01; Zeedijk 1; ⏰ 3pm-1am Mon-Thu, 3pm-3am Fri & Sat; 🚊 4/9/16/24/25 Centraal Station

Candles burn even during the day at this super-*gezellig* (p160) bar in a 15th-century house, one of two remaining wooden buildings in the city. (The other's in the Begijnhof, p40). Vintage jazz on the stereo enhances the time-warp feel. The name allegedly comes from the bar's role in the 16th and 17th centuries as a crash pad for sailors from the Far East, who often toted *aapjes* (monkeys) with them.

▼ KADINSKY *Coffeeshop*
☎ 624 70 23; Rosmarijnsteeg 9; ⏰ 10am-1am Mon-Fri, 10am-2am Sat & Sun; 🚊 1/2/5 Spui

On the surface this could be an actual *coffee* shop – there's no trace of hippy grunge, just sleek minimalist furniture, cool electronica in the background, and good java and hot chocolate. Three levels offer various cosy nooks. Two much smaller branches are at Langebrugsteeg 7a and Zoutsteeg 14.

▼ LATEI *Cafe*
☎ 625 74 85; Zeedijk 143; ⏰ 8am-6pm Mon-Wed, 8am-10pm Thu & Fri, 9am-10pm Sat, 11am-6pm Sun; 🚊 4/9/16/24/25 Dam; Ⓥ ♿

Don't worry, the cool staff at this tiny cafe won't sell the Formica-top table out from under you – though it, and every other piece of mod decor is, for sale. A steady stream of neighbourhood residents pops in for *koffie verkeerd* (milky coffee).

▼ LIME *Lounge*
☎ 639 30 20; Zeedijk 104;
🚊 4/9/16/24/25 Dam

A rare hip lounge in this area, Lime has all the right style elements: a mod orange-and-brown interior, cool club music on the hi-fi and good cocktails (rare anywhere in Amsterdam), which are just €5 between 5pm and 10pm.

▼ 'T MANDJE
Gay & Lesbian, Brown Cafe
☎ 622 53 75; Zeedijk 63;
🚊 4/9/16/24/25 Centraal Station

Amsterdam's – and perhaps the world's – oldest gay bar opened in 1927, then shut in 1982, when the Zeedijk grew too seedy. But its trinket-covered interior was lovingly dusted every week until it reopened in 2008. The devoted bartenders can tell you stories about the bar's brassy lesbian founder, and there's live jazz and a retro DJ who spins 78s on a Victrola. One of the most *gezellig* places in the Centrum, gay or straight.

▼ VAN ZUYLEN *Brown Cafe*
☎ 639 10 55; Torensteeg 4; 🕐 10am-1am Sun-Thu, 10am-3am Fri & Sat;
🚊 1/2/5/13/14/17 Raadhuisstraat

Although the sunny terrace is one of the prettiest spots for a drink on the Singel, the interior – with its rooms featuring lots of wood and

old leather banquettes – is just as appealing in the cooler months.

▼ VRANKRIJK *Bar*
Spuistraat 216; 🕐 from 9pm;
🚊 1/2/5/14 Paleisstraat

Squatters keep it real at this grungy, graffiti-covered and very cheap bar, which functions as a social-support centre for Amsterdam's various subcultures. Monday is always Queer Night, Thursday is for punks and Saturday usually sees some sweaty dancing.

▼ WIJNAND FOCKINK
Tasting House
☎ 639 26 95; Pijlsteeg 31; 🕐 3-9pm;
🚊 4/9/16/24/25 Dam

The crowd gets boisterous in this 1679 tasting room, despite the early closing time and the admonition over the door: 'Shh…the *jenever* is resting.' The distillery is also open for tours from 9am to 5pm weekdays and 1pm to 6pm Saturday.

⭐ PLAY

⭐ BITTERZOET *Live Music*
☎ 521 30 01; www.bitterzoet.com, in Dutch; Spuistraat 2; 🚊 1/2/5/13/17 Martelaarsgracht

This small but versatile venue keeps a fresh attitude with a calendar that includes Afrobeat, Latin, hip hop and old-school jazz. We have received a couple of reports of a tourist-hostile attitude at the door, though we haven't noticed this in person.

☆ CASA ROSSO *Sex Show*

☎ 627 89 43; www.janot.com; Oudezijds Achterburgwal 106-108; admission €30; ⏰ 8pm-2am Sun-Thu, 8pm-3am Fri & Sat; 🚊 4/9/16/24/25 Dam

It might be stretching it to describe a live sex show as 'classy', but this theatre is clean and comfortable and always packed with couples and hen's-night parties. We miss the penis fountain out front – look instead for the giant pink elephant sign.

☆ CASABLANCA

Live Music, Theatre

☎ 625 56 85; www.casablanca -amsterdam.nl, in Dutch; Zeedijk 24; 🚊 4/9/16/24/25 Centraal Station

Split-personality Casablanca once had a hot reputation for jazz (combos still take the stage early in the week), but now it's better known as a karaoke madhouse on the weekends. Next door at No 26 is Casablanca Varieté, an intimate cabaret-style theatre where Dutch drag queens, magicians and more take the stage every night but Monday, for just a €5 cover charge.

☆ WINSTON KINGDOM

Live Music

☎ 623 13 80; www.winston.nl; Warmoesstraat 129; 🚊 4/9/16/24/25 Dam

Something about being in a small space with a loud band makes people drink *a lot*. No matter what's on – from Brazilian DJs to Elvis Costello cover bands – the scene can get pretty wild in this grungy little club. Check the website for agenda details.

>JORDAAN & WESTERN CANALS

First dug in the 17th century, the Grachtengordel (Canal Belt) offered bigger lots for wealthy businessmen to live in the style they deserved – and it's still the city's best address. Many grand old mansions here are now offices, schools and exhibition space, but the wide, watery avenues retain a sedate, residential feel. (Mnemonic tip: Herengracht, Keizersgracht and Prinsengracht are in alphabetical order as you head out from the centre.) The single-block cross-streets that link them are livelier and packed with quirky shops and cafes – most famously in the Negen Straatjes (Nine Streets, p14) area south of Raadhuisstraat, but also to the north.

Due west of the canals is the Jordaan, a neighbourhood with working-class roots. Old-time residents are proud of their distinctive accent, their romantic music (*levenslied*, the tears-in-your-beer ballad style, flourishes here) and a checkered history that includes an 1886 brawl with the police that started with a greased-eel-pulling contest. The neighbourhood has weathered extreme gentrification, beginning in the early 20th century when tenements were razed up to the 1980s when it became the city's hot district, but it hasn't lost its tight-knit village feel. So while there's an olive-oil boutique and many art galleries, there are also second-hand clothing stores and lace curtains, even in the windows of generic 1980s rebuilds. With a charming small bar on nearly every corner, the Jordaan is a font of *gezelligheid* (p160).

Bordering both neighbourhoods on the north is Haarlemmerstraat and Haarlemmerdijk – one long, busy shopping street with a hipper edge, and lots of places to snack or relax over a drink.

JORDAAN & WESTERN CANALS

🔵 SEE

🟠 SHOP

🍴 EAT

🍷 DRINK

⭐ PLAY

Please see over for map

◉ SEE

◉ ANNE FRANK HUIS

☎ 556 71 05; www.annefrank
.org; Prinsengracht 267; adult/child
under 10yr/child 10-17yr €7.50/free/
3.50; ⏰ 9am-9pm Sun-Fri, 9am-10pm
Sat mid-Mar–mid-Sep, 9am-7pm Sat
mid-Sep–mid-Mar, closed Yom Kippur;
🚊 13/14/17 Westermarkt; ♿

The Anne Frank Huis (p11), where
the teenage diarist hid with her
family during WWII, receives
nearly a million visitors a year. To
skip the queue, buy tickets online;
the next best option is to show
up early or late, or on a very drizzly day. The line moves steadily,
though, as it takes only about 45
minutes to tour the house and the
adjacent exhibits.

◉ BIJBELS MUSEUM

☎ 624 24 36; www.bijbelsmuseum
.nl; Herengracht 366-368; admission
€7.50/3.75; ⏰ 10am-5pm Mon-Sat,
11am-5pm Sun; 🚊 1/2/5 Spui

Not just a museum of Bibles, this
canal house trove is more like a
museum of the importance of the
Bible in 19th-century culture. It
contains musty mummies, hand-
carved models of the Tabernacle
and the Temple in Jerusalem, as
well as some antique Bibles. Near
the pretty garden, there's also a
display of biblical smells (nicer
than it sounds).

◉ HOUSEBOAT MUSEUM

☎ 427 07 50; www.houseboat
museum.nl; opposite Prinsengracht 296;
admission €3.25/2.50; ⏰ 11am-5pm
Tue-Sun Mar-Oct, 11am-5pm Fri-Sun
Nov-Feb, closed Jan; 🚊 13/14/17
Westermarkt

If you're curious how people live
on a *woonboot* (houseboat), then
check out the quarters on the
Hendrika Maria, a former commercial ship built in 1914. There's
a short video presentation on the
varieties of houseboats, but the
really interesting part is just feeling an apartment rock beneath
your feet.

◉ HUIS MARSEILLE

☎ 531 89 89; www.huismarseille
.nl; Keizersgracht 401; admission
€5/3; ⏰ 11am-6pm Tue-Sun; 🚊 1/2/5
Keizersgracht

Whether you prefer this contemporary photography museum or
FOAM (p81) depends largely on
what is showing. But the setting
here is lovelier, with exhibitions of
international work in five spacious
rooms complete with 18th-century
details, and a tiny summerhouse in
the garden. There's a terrific little
library too.

◉ POEZENBOOT

☎ 625 87 94; across from Singel
40; ⏰ 1-3pm Thu-Tue; 🚊 1/2/5/13/17
Martelaarsgracht

Soft-hearted visitors might think twice before stopping by the 'cat boat', a houseboat specially made for stray cats. They've all been spayed or neutered, and are looking oh-so-ready for adoption.

⊙ STEDELIJK MUSEUM BUREAU AMSTERDAM

☎ 422 04 71; www.smba.nl; Rozenstraat 59; admission free; ⏰ 11am-5pm Tue-Sun; ⓣ 13/14/17 Westermarkt

While the Stedelijk Museum (p98) is undergoing its restoration, this is its only other permanent outlet. It doesn't display works from the Stedelijk collection, but instead mounts new works in installation, photography, design and new media.

⊙ THEATERMUSEUM

☎ 551 33 00; www.tin.nl; Herengracht 168; admission €4.50/2.25; ⏰ 11am-5pm Mon-Fri, 1-5pm Sat & Sun; ⓣ 13/14/17 Westermarkt

Two canal houses – one is the majestic Bartolotti House, built by the same architect who designed the Westerkerk (right) – display costumes, set models, and posters and photos. The exhibits aren't huge on narrative, but there is a rather nifty installation of a 'chamber theatre' with its complex system of changing backdrops, as well as a very nice garden and cafe.

GABLE STONES

Before street numbers were introduced in 1795, many Amsterdam homes were identified by a painted or carved stone plaque above the doorway. Beautiful examples of these gable stones are still in place particularly in the Jordaan, and salvaged ones have been installed outside the Amsterdam's Historisch Museum (p40) and in the Begijnhof (p40). Occupations are a frequent theme – tobacconists, skippers, even undertakers. Animals are also popular: the bar De Kat in de Wijngaert (p73) takes its name, The Cat in the Vineyard, from its gable stone. Modern buildings sometimes get a new old-style plaque – there's a particularly clever one at Lindengracht 55.

⊙ WESTERKERK

☎ 624 77 66; www.westerkerk.nl; Prinsengracht 281; entry free, tower €6; ⏰ church 11am-3pm Mon-Sat Apr-Oct, tower 10am-5pm Mon-Sat Apr-Sep; ⓣ 13/14/17 Westermarkt

Though it's technically not in the Jordaan, this massive Protestant church, built in 1631, has become a symbol of the neighbourhood. Its 85m-high tower is the city's tallest. To be a true *jordaner*, it's said, you must be born within earshot of the Westerkerk's carillon bells and, according to church records, Rembrandt lies here, in an unmarked pauper's grave. Climbing the tower reveals a fine view, but

NEIGHBOURHOODS

JORDAAN & WESTERN CANALS

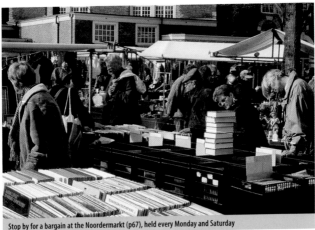
Stop by for a bargain at the Noordermarkt (p67), held every Monday and Saturday

it's not for the faint-hearted – there's a perceptible sway in windy weather.

🏠 SHOP

🏠 & KLEVERING *Housewares*
☎ 422 27 08; Haarlemmerstraat 8; 🚊 1/2/5/13/17 Martelaarsgracht
A branch of the nifty shop near Vondelpark (p99).

🏠 ANTONIA BY YVETTE *Footwear*
☎ 320 94 43; Herengracht 243; 🕑 Tue-Sat; 🚊 1/2/5/14 Paleisstraat
A wonderland of footwear for men and women, which overflows into the building next door: stilettos, boots, espadrilles and even house slippers, from an assortment of international brands.

🏠 BOEKIE WOEKIE *Books*
☎ 639 05 07; Berenstraat 16; 🕑 noon-6pm; 🚊 13/14/17 Westermarkt
Essentially an art gallery, except the works here are all books by artists, whether that means a self-published monograph or an illustrated story that's handcrafted right down to the paper.

🏠 BRILMUSEUM *Eyeglasses*
☎ 421 24 14; Gasthuismolensteeg 7; 🕑 11.30am-5.30pm Wed-Fri, 11.30am-5pm Sat; 🚊 1/2/5/14 Paleisstraat

The Museum of Spectacles displays 700 years' worth of glasses and sells unworn vintage frames, for anyone who wants to look like Jackie O or Buddy Holly.

☐ DE LOOIER *Antiques*
☎ 624 90 38; Elandsgracht 109; ◐ 11am-5pm Sat-Thu; ⓧ 7/10/17 **Elandsgracht**

Anyone with an affinity for odd antiques and bric-a-brac may enter this knick-knack minimall and never come out. You're just as likely to find 1940s silk dresses as you are 1970s Swedish porn.

☐ DE WITTE TANDEN WINKEL *Speciality Shop*
☎ 623 34 43; Runstraat 5; ◐ Mon-Sat; ⓧ 1/2/5 **Spui**

We love shops that are obsessed, and the 'White-Teeth Shop' certainly is – with dental hygiene. Pop in here for toothbrushes, toothpastes from around the world and brushing accessories you never knew you needed.

☐ ENGLISH BOOKSHOP *Books*
☎ 626 42 30; Lauriergracht 71; ◐ Tue-Sat; ⓧ 7/10/17 **Elandsgracht**

Stocked with the best range of Dutch literature and books on Amsterdam available in English, this is a great place to browse. It also features an excellent contemporary fiction section and a basement full of children's books.

☐ EVA DAMAVE *Clothing*
☎ 627 73 25; 2e Laurierdwarsstraat 51c; ◐ noon-6pm Wed-Sat; ⓧ 10/13/14/17 **Marnixstraat**

Wool is the medium for this designer, who weaves punchy sweaters, shawls and dresses. Some of the patchwork styles are a bit too 'Cosby sweater' for our tastes, but the striped pieces are subtle and beautiful, and usually one-of-a-kind.

☐ FROZEN FOUNTAIN *Design*
☎ 622 93 75; Prinsengracht 629; ◐ Tue-Sat; ⓧ 1/2/5 **Prinsengracht**

These two canal houses are crammed full of the cleverest, coolest home design you're likely to come across, most of it Dutch. You can spend thousands on a curlicue radiator, but there is a variety of more accessible items, such as clever takes on Dutch bar towels.

☐ HESTER VAN EEGHEN *Footwear*
☎ 626 92 11; Hartenstraat 1; ◐ Tue-Sat; ⓧ 13/14/17 **Westermarkt**

For her transfixing footwear, Van Eeghen applies bright solid colours to classic shapes – apple-green ankle boots, curvaceous red-and-pink pumps. Her handbags and wallets, just down the street at No 37, are just as attention grabbing.

DROP IT LIKE IT'S HOT

The Dutch love their lollies, the most famous of which is *drop*, the word for all varieties of liquorice. It may be gummy-soft or tough as leather, shaped like coins or miniature cars, but the most important distinction is between *zoete* (sweet) and *zoute* (salty, also called *salmiak*). The latter is often an alarming surprise, even for avowed fans of the black stuff. But with such a range of textures and additional flavours – mint, honey, laurel – even liquorice-sceptics might be converted. Het Oud-Hollandsche Snoepwinkeltje (below) is a good place to do a taste test.

🏠 HET OUD-HOLLANDSCH SNOEPWINKELTJE
Food & Drink

☎ 420 73 90; 2e Egelantiersdwarsstraat 2; 🚊 3/10 Marnixplein
Look out for stampeding children before you reach for the door at this tiny corner shop filled floor to ceiling with sweets (and more than just liquorice), most sold in bulk from big glass jars.

🏠 HJ VAN DE KERKHOF
Speciality Shop

☎ 623 46 66; Wolvenstraat 9-11; 🚊 13/14/17 Westermarkt
One of the Negen Straatje's most delightful old-fashioned stores, Kerkhof deals exclusively in passementerie: lace ribbon, rickrack, silk cord, curtain tassels. Surely *something* you own needs a little trim?

🏠 JG BEUNE *Food & Drink*

☎ 624 83 56; Haarlemmerdijk 156-58; 🕑 Tue-Sat; 🚊 3 Haarlemmerplein
This chandelier-bedecked sweet shop has been making pastries and chocolate since 1882. One speciality is a box of chocolates in the shape of *amsterdammertjes*, the bollards that line city side-walks – a great gift, if you can keep yourself from eating it.

🏠 KITSCH KITCHEN
Housewares

☎ 622 82 61; Rozengracht 8-12; 🚊 13/14/17 Westermarkt
No wonder this shop is so popular in cloudy Amsterdam: everywhere you lay your eyes is vibrant colour. Mexican flower-print vinyl sheeting is transformed into everything from bibs to bike bags, and there's also aluminium Thai soup bowls, groovy melamine plates and plenty more to liven up your home.

🏠 LA SAVONNERIE
Perfume & Cosmetics

☎ 428 11 39; Prinsengracht 294; 🕑 Mon-Sat; 🚊 13/14/17 Westermarkt
Aromatic La Savonnerie is stocked with wonderful soaps from around the world, from Aleppo to Belgium.

But the real star is the rainbowlike display of 80 or so soaps made in-house, with beautiful natural scents.

🏠 LAURA DOLS *Clothing*
☎ 624 90 66; Wolvenstraat 7;
🚋 13/14/17 Westermarkt

Some of the finest vintage clothing in the Netherlands – head here if you like your retro style glamorous, not campy. A shop across the street (No 6) handles the overflow, plus a line of home linens made from old-fashioned Dutch farm textiles.

🏠 MARLIES DEKKERS *Clothing*
☎ 421 19 00; Berenstraat 18;
🚋 13/14/17 Westermarkt

A branch of the Dutch lingerie queen (see p100).

🏠 MIAUW *Clothing*
☎ 422 05 61; Hartenstraat 36;
🚋 13/14/17 Westermarkt

Analik is one of Amsterdam's edgier designers, and her shop showcases both her own idiosyncratic work and that of likeminded European labels. It also houses changing exhibitions of graffiti, and graphic and conceptual art.

🏠 MONO *Clothing*
☎ 427 10 89; Haarlemmerstraat 16;
🕙 11am-5.30pm Mon-Fri, 11am-6pm Sat; 🚋 1/2/5/13/17 Martelaarsgracht

The owners of this little shop got their start at the Waterlooplein,

selling sturdy canvas bags in groovy prints. It sounds like a contradiction in terms, but they even design very cool bumbags.

🏠 NOORDERMARKT
Clothing, Food & Drink
🕙 8am-1pm Mon, 9am-3pm Sat;
🚋 3 Nieuwe Willemsstraat

The square in front of the Noorderkerk hosts two markets: on Monday mornings, it's a trove of second-hand clothing (great rummage piles) and assorted antique trinkets, and on Saturdays, most (but not all) of the clothing stalls are replaced by gorgeous produce and cheese from organic growers around Amsterdam.

🏠 PAPABUBBLE *Food & Drink*
☎ 626 26 62; Haarlemmerdijk 70;
🕙 Mon-Sat; 🚋 3 Haarlemmerplein

This hip lolly shop looks more like a gallery. There's performance art too – pull up a cushion and perch on the stairs to watch the mesmerising process of transforming sugar into gemlike sweets with flavours like pomelo and lavender.

🏠 SHIRDAK
Clothing, Housewares
☎ 626 68 00; Prinsengracht 192;
🕙 11am-5.30pm Mon-Fri, 10am-5pm Sat; 🚋 13/14/17 Westermarkt

Wooden clogs not for you? Pick up a pair of beautiful soft felt ones here, complete with whimsically curled toes. It also stocks felt clothing and blankets, as well as African, Chinese and Central Asian textiles.

🛒 SPRMRKT Clothing, Design
☎ 330 56 01; Rozengracht 191-193;
🚊 10/13/14/17 Marnixstraat
Whether you want a super-tight pair of Acne jeans, a vintage Thor Larsen Pod chair or the latest copy of *Butt* magazine, it's at this industrial-feeling concept store, a major player in Amsterdam's fashion scene.

🛍 VAN RAVENSTEIN
Clothing
☎ 639 00 67; www.van-ravenstein .nl; Keizersgracht 359; ⏰ 1-6pm Mon, 11am-6pm Tue-Sat; 🚊 1/2/5 Spui
The shop itself is minimalist, but all the better to show off all the big names in Dutch and Flemish fashion, such as Viktor & Rolf, Ann Demeulemeester and Dries Van Noten – but then who can resist a little Givenchy on the side?

📷 YOUR CUP OF T
Clothing
☎ 420 71 53; Westerstraat 77;
⏰ 10am-2pm Mon, 2-7pm Wed-Fri, noon-6pm Sat; 🚊 3/10 Marnixplein
Design your own souvenir T-shirt at this tiny basement shop, where you can browse through a million

iron-on graphics and letters. Undecided? Fluorescent robots are a timeless option.

🍴 EAT

🍴 BALTHAZAR'S KEUKEN
Mediterranean €€
☎ 420 21 14; Elandsgracht 108; ⏰ 6-11pm Wed-Fri; 🚊 7/10/17 Elandsgracht
This restaurant offers a fixed-price, three-course menu that changes weekly. With an open kitchen and only a few tables, it feels like eating at someone's house. It's only open three days a week so make sure you book ahead.

🍴 BLUE PEPPER
Indonesian €€€
☎ 489 70 39; Nassaukade 366; ⏰ 6-10pm; 🚊 7/10 Raamplein; V
Too often, Indonesian food is little more than a hangover treatment. Chef Sonja elevates the cuisine to art, adds other Pacific Rim references and serves the results in a dramatic black dining room.

🍴 BORDEWIJK French €€€
☎ 624 38 99; Noordermarkt 7; ⏰ dinner Tue-Sun; 🚊 3 Nieuwe Willemsstraat
The chef at Bordewijk, one of the city's best French restaurants, is confident enough in his stellar food – rustic pâté, marrow bones, garlicky *bourride* – that he doesn't need to dress up the spare dining room with chandeliers or velvet

banquettes. In summer, there are tables on the canal.

🍴 BROODJE MOKUM
Sandwich Shop €

☎ 623 19 66; Rozengracht 26; ⏰ 8am-3pm Mon-Sat; 🚊 13/14/17 Westermarkt
Great sandwiches – just point and they'll tell you the price. More so than at most other *broodje* shops, there's room to sit down and spread out.

🍴 BUFFET VAN ODETTE
Cafe €

☎ 423 60 34; Herengracht 309; ⏰ 8.30am-4.30pm Mon & Wed-Fri, 10am-5.30pm Sat & Sun; 🚊 1/2/5 Spui; V ♿
It's hard to get a seat in this tiny place on the weekend – it's packed with customers noshing on fat meatloaf sandwiches and omelettes with truffle cheese. Stay for sweets too: the sticky toffee and carrot cakes are delicious.

🍴 DE BELHAMEL *French* €€

☎ 622 10 95; Brouwersgracht 60; ⏰ dinner; 🚊 1/2/5/13/17 Martelaarsgracht; V
A beautiful restaurant on a beautiful canal: the gorgeous art nouveau dining room takes on an almost palpable glow in the evenings. The food, while not quite as memorable as the scenery, does some neat hopping between

French, Italian and Dutch, with excellent seafood.

🍴 DE BOLHOED
Vegetarian €€

☎ 626 18 03; Prinsengracht 60-62; ⏰ lunch & dinner; 🚊 13/14/17 Westermarkt; V ♿
An old-school veggie eatery, De Bolhoed has been dishing up generous helpings of Italian, Mexican and Middle Eastern dishes to Amsterdammers for decades. Arrive early for the vegan special.

🍴 DE KAASKAMER
Delicatessen €

☎ 623 34 83; Runstraat 7; 🚊 1/2/5 Spui
This wonderful cheese shop is the best in town for Dutch varieties, and also stocks olives, tapenades, salads and other picnic ingredients. You try before you buy, and they're happy to make up cheese baskets to take home.

🍴 DIVAN *Turkish* €€

☎ 626 82 39; Elandsgracht 14; ⏰ 5-11pm; 🚊 13/14/17 Westermarkt; V ♿
Though it looks like a standard brown cafe, this great little restaurant is one of Amsterdam's best Turkish restaurants, with exceptionally sweet service. Order some *meze* (mixed starters) and don't miss out on the lamb as a main course.

NEIGHBOURHOODS

JORDAAN & WESTERN CANALS

🍴 FESTINA LENTE
Cafe   €€

☎ 638 14 12; Looiersgracht 40b; noon-1am Sun & Mon, 10.30am-1am Tue-Thu, 10.30am-3am Fri & Sat; 🚋 7/10/17 Elandsgracht; 👶 Ⓥ

This neighbourhood hangout is typical Jordaan *gezelligheid*, packed with regulars snacking on small-portion Mediterranean dishes and big sandwiches named after famous writers.

🍴 FOODISM
International   €€

☎ 427 51 03; Oude Leliestraat 8; 🕓 11.30am-10pm Mon-Fri, 12.30-6pm Sat & Sun; 🚋 1/2/5/13/17 Raadhuisstraat; Ⓥ 👶

A good all-day cafe with friendly staff, Foodism serves up big breakfasts, filling sandwiches (try the goat cheese and chorizo) and hearty, handmade pastas. A good selection of vegetarian dishes too.

🍴 LOS PILONES
Mexican   €€

☎ 620 0323; 1e Anjeliersdwarsstraat 6; 🕓 4-11.30pm Tue-Sun; 🚋 3/10 Marnixplein; Ⓥ 👶

A branch of the Mexican place on Kerkstraat (p88).

🍴 MERCAN *Turkish*   €

☎ 638 01 65; Rozengracht 148; 🕓 8am-5pm; 🚋 10/13/14/17 Marnixstraat; Ⓥ 👶

This Turkish bakery is an excellent pit stop for a *turkse pizza* – aka *lahmacun*, a crispy flatbread topped with spiced ground meat, creamy yoghurt and hot sauce and rolled up for easy eating.

🍴 MOEDERS *Dutch*   €€

☎ 626 79 57; Rozengracht 251; 🕓 dinner; 🚋 10/13/14/17 Marnixstraat; Ⓥ 👶

'Mothers' is stocked with customers' own plates, flatware and photos of their mums, and the result is a delightful hotchpotch. So is the food, including seafood, Moroccan dishes, a vegetarian frittata and a *rijsttafel*-style presentation of traditional Dutch dishes in many small plates.

🍴 PANCAKES! *Dutch*   €

☎ 528 97 97; Berenstraat 38; 🕓 10am-7pm; 🚋 13/14/17 Westermarkt; Ⓥ 👶

A great place to sample Dutch pancakes in an atmosphere free of clogs and other kitsch – and there are just as many locals here as tourists. All the usual options, plus daily creations like aubergine, chicory and cheese, grace the menu.

🍴 POMPADOUR
Bakery & Sweets   €

☎ 623 95 54; Huidenstraat 12; 🕓 9.30am-5.45pm Mon-Fri, 9am-5.30pm Sat; 🚋 1/2/5 Spui

At this little gold-wallpapered patisserie, join society ladies

Klary Koopmans
Food blogger at Alles Over Eten (All About Food, www.klarykoopmans.com)

Favourite kind of liquorice I don't actually like *drop* (p66) much. Not typical, I know, but I prefer savoury foods, like herring. **Fish facts** How the shop handles the herring makes the biggest difference – the fish should be cleaned just before you eat it. If you see a big stack of prepared fish, that's not good. Go to the places with fast turnover. Also, the very little bones don't look so nice, sticking out of the sandwich, but you can eat them. **Authentic snack** Go to Van Dobben (p90) and have a *broodje kroket* (croquette sandwich). It's very Amsterdam, with the busyness and people talking across the counter. **Save your money** There are a lot of midrange, trying-too-hard restaurants here. You're much better off going for cheap Turkish or Surinamese, and saving for a big splurge, like at Marius (p78) or Le Hollandais (p110).

After perusing the Noodermarkt, settle down for an afternoon pastry or cake

sipping top-notch tea and nib-
bling at the Frenchiest cakes in
town. The handmade chocolates
are tasty too, and you can get
them to go.

🍴 SEMHAR *Ethiopian* €€
☎ 638 16 34; Marnixstraat 259-261;
⏱ 1-11pm Tue-Sun; 🚊 10 Bloemgracht; V &
Yohannes gives his customers a
warm welcome, and he's a fanatic
about the quality of his *injera*
bread – all the better to sop up
richly spiced stews and vegetable combos. We always skip the
menu and just ask for a mixed
platter.

🍴 SPANJER EN VAN TWIST
Cafe €€
☎ 639 01 09; Leliegracht 60;
⏱ 10am-10pm Sun-Thu, 10am-11pm Fri
& Sat; 🚊 13/14/17 Westermarkt; &
Just north of the Anne Frank Huis,
Spanjer en Van Twist's tables on
Leliegracht are great for watching
the boats cruise by. The eclectic
lunch and dinner menu is perfectly good, but it's a really great place
for an afternoon pastry or cake.

🍴 STOUT *Cafe* €€
☎ 616 36 64; Haarlemmerstraat 73;
⏱ 10am-11pm Mon-Sat, noon-11pm Sun;
🚊 1/2/5/13/17 Martelaarsgracht; V
A slick crowd congregates to
read design magazines and share

fusion dishes, such as carrot and coriander soup with spicy tempeh and Thai chicken burger with kimchi, and fruit shakes. Fitting for the name (*stout* means 'naughty' in Dutch), flirting seems to be a primary activity here.

🍴 UNLIMITED DELICIOUS
Bakery & Sweets   €
☎ 622 48 29; Haarlemmerstraat 122;
🕒 Mon-Sat; 🚊 1/2/5/13/17
Martelaarsgracht
It's certainly tempting to dive into the gorgeous, sculptural cakes and tarts, but don't fill up before you get to the home-made chocolates. The fruit-chocolate combos are intense. You can either sit down and enjoy your selections with a coffee, or pack it all up to take away.

🍴 WIL GRAANSTRA FRITESHUIS *Fast Food*   €
☎ 624 40 71; Westermarkt 11;
🕒 11am-6pm; 🚊 13/14/17
Westermarkt; ♿ Ⓥ 👶
This little stall near the Anne Frank Huis has been serving up fries with mayo since 1956. They're an almost eerie shade of gold, and delectably light and crispy.

🍴 WINKEL 43 *Cafe*   €
☎ 623 02 23; Noordermarkt 43;
🕒 breakfast, lunch & dinner; 🚊 3
Nieuwe Willemsstraat; 👶

This sprawling space serves meals, but most people come here just for its tall, cakey apple pie. You'd best not get a hankering for it on market days (Mondays and Saturdays), as there's almost always a queue out the door.

🍸 DRINK

🍸 BARNEY'S *Coffeeshop*
☎ 625 97 61; Haarlemmerstraat 102;
🕒 7am-8pm; 🚊 1/2/5/13/17
Martelaarsgracht
Barney's got famous on bargain English breakfasts all day, along with the marijuana. A new focus has vastly improved Barney's weed, but unfortunately shunted the breakfasts across the street to the smoke-friendly Barney's Lounge – handy, but not as cheap-and-cheerful as in days of yore, and only open until 3pm.

🍸 DE KAT IN DE WIJNGAERT
Brown Cafe
☎ 620 45 54; Lindengracht 160;
🚊 3 Nieuwe Willemsstraat
Rivalling 't Smalle (p76) for overwhelming *gezelligheid,* this gorgeous bar is the kind of place where one beer soon turns to half a dozen – maybe it's the bad influence of the old-guard arts types who hang out here. At least you can soak it all up with what many people vote as the best *tosti* (toasted sandwich) in town.

▼ DE KOE *Bar*
☎ 625 44 82; Marnixstraat 381; 🚊 7/10 Raamplein

With a pinball machine, darts, board games and good cheap meals on hand, you'll never get bored at 'the Cow', a casual spot not far from the Leidseplein.

▼ DE PELS *Brown Cafe*
☎ 622 90 37; Huidenstraat 25; 🚊 1/2/5 Spui

The action at this appealingly shabby *bruin café* is focused on reading the newspaper and drinking. It's also a Sunday morning breakfast favourite.

▼ DE TWEE ZWAANTJES *Brown Cafe*
☎ 625 27 29; Prinsengracht 114; 🚊 13/14/17 Westermarkt

At this bar, crooners with big hair and ruffled shirts belt out nostalgic anthems with accordion accompaniment. Come here if you're sick of trendy lounges, and sing along if you can: *Oh Amsterdam, wat ben je mooi…* ('Oh Amsterdam, how beautiful you are… '). In summer, karaoke replaces the pros.

▼ DE ZOTTE *Beer Bar*
☎ 626 86 94; Raamstraat 29; 🚊 7/10 Raamplein

If you can't make up your mind in this Belgian beer bar, start with the weekly special. Those Trappist monks can brew some deadly ones so you might want to line your stomach with a hearty cheese plate or steak – the kitchen's open between 6.30pm and 9pm.

▼ FINCH *Cafe*
☎ 626 24 61; Noordermarkt 5; 🕑 9am-1am Sun-Thu, 9am-3am Fri & Sat; 🚊 3 Nieuwe Willemsstraat

This funky cafe-lounge is one of the major hangouts for more stylish Jordaan residents. When equally cool Proust bar next door also gets going, the place just hums.

▼ GREY AREA *Coffeeshop*
☎ 420 43 01; Oude Leliestraat 2; 🕑 noon-8pm; 🚊 1/2/5/13/17 Raadhuisstraat

Owned by a couple of guys from the US, this tiny shop plastered with band and skateboard stickers doles out specialities like 'Double Bubble-Gum' to regular customers. It also keeps up the American tradition of coffee refills (it's organic).

▼ HET MOLENPAD *Brown Cafe*
☎ 625 96 80; Prinsengracht 653; 🕑 noon-1am Sun-Thu, noon-2am Fri & Sat; 🚊 1/2/5 Prinsengracht

The canalside terrace here is so prime for catching the afternoon sun that, to be honest, we've never noticed what the inside looks like. The snack plates are super for sharing with friends.

Y LA TERTULIA *Coffeeshop*
☎ 623 85 03; Prinsengracht 312;
🕐 11am-7pm Tue-Sat; 🚇 7/10/17
Elandsgracht
This plant-filled canalside spot
is great for a sunny-day smoke.
The weed selection is limited, so
you might want to just treat it as
a stoner-friendly cafe, complete
with delicious juices, herbal teas
and toasted sandwiches.

Y ROKERIJ *Coffeeshop*
☎ 626 30 60; Elandsgracht 53;
🚇 7/10/17 Elandsgracht
An all-Indian-theme branch of the
Leidseplein operation (p91). Yet
another, at Singel 8, has an even
trippier interior.

Y SAAREIN II *Gay & Lesbian*
☎ 623 49 01; Elandsstraat 119;
🕐 4pm-1am Tue-Thu & Sun, 4pm-2am Fri,
noon-2am Sat; 🚇 7/10/17 Elandsgracht
Saarein was a focal point for the
feminist movement in the 1970s
and had a strict women-only policy. It has since relaxed its policies a
bit, and bills itself as a 'mixed gay
cafe', though the crowd still skews
female.

Y SANEMENTERENG
Coffeeshop
☎ 624 19 07; 2e Laurierdwarsstraat 44;
🚇 10/13/14/17 Marnixstraat
One minute you're picking
through second-hand trinkets
on the pavement outside. Next
minute you're buying a chipped
delftware plate and a gram of out-
door-grown ganja, and grooving
to the strains of 'Legalise It'. Hours
can be erratic, but it usually opens
around 2pm.

Y SIMON LÉVELT *Cafe*
☎ 624 08 23; Prinsengracht 180;
🕐 10am-6pm Mon-Fri, 10am-5pm Sat,
1-5pm Sun; 🚇 13/14/17 Westermarkt
For more than two centuries,
Lévelt has been selling tea and

GO WEST?
'West is the new Centrum' boasts **Club 8** (☎ 685 17 03; www.club-8.nl, in Dutch; Admiraal de Ruijterweg 56b; 🚇 12/13/14 Admiraal de Ruijterweg), a bare-bones club in
the area west of the Jordaan. We wouldn't write off the city centre anytime soon, but
we can say that this and other grassroots nightspots here are worth a look: **De Nieuwe
Anita** (☎ 064-150 35 12; www.denieuweanita.nl, in Dutch; Frederik Hendrikstraat 111;
🚇 3 Hugo de Grootplein), a living-room-like art lounge; **Zaal 100** (☎ 688 01 27;
www.zaal100.nl; De Wittenstraat 100; 🚇 10 De Wittenkade), which hosts a Tuesday
jam session; and the multicultural arts space **Podium Mozaïek** (☎ 580 03 80; www
.podiummozaiek.nl; Bos en Lommerweg 191; 🚇 12/14 Bos en Lommerweg).

coffee in the Netherlands. This is its original shopfront, and it has a beautiful little garden out the back.

▼ SOUND GARDEN *Bar*
☎ 620 28 53; Marnixstraat 164-66; 🚋 10/13/14/17 Marnixstraat

The grunge-era name is no coincidence – the soundtrack at this roomy, ramshackle bar tends towards ragged indie rock. But there is a genuine garden – a large terrace out back on the canal. Pinball and cheap drinks are bonuses.

▼ STRUIK *Bar & Cafe*
Rozengracht 160; 🚋 10/13/14/17 Marnixstraat

If you prefer your beer with a background of hip hop, breakbeats and soul, come to this laid-back corner cafe, which does good food (rockin' roti on Tuesdays, hangover brunch on Sundays) then segues into drinking and chatting to an old-school playlist or a DJ on weekends.

▼ 'T SMALLE *Brown Cafe*
☎ 623 96 17; Egelantiersgracht 12; 🕒 10am-1am; 🚋 13/14/17 Westermarkt

Patrons enjoying a splash of Amsterdam's fickle sunshine at Finch (p74)

There's no more convivial spot than this canalside terrace on a sunny day and the 18th-century interior is perfect in winter. Proof of its powerful *gezelligheid*, it manages to remain a lively local bar even while being gushed over in almost every guidebook in print.

VYNE *Wine Bar*

☎ 344 64 08; Prinsengracht 411; ⏰ 6pm-midnight Mon-Thu, 5pm-1am Fri & Sat, 4-11pm Sun; 🚊 13/14/17 Westermarkt; ♿ Ⓥ

This sleek space is one of the few wine bars in town. It does a particularly great job of pairing snacks with every variety of vino, and we especially recommend the Love Bites – fancy-flavoured, all-vegetarian *bitterballen* (minicroquettes).

WOLVENSTRAAT *Cafe*

☎ 320 08 43; Wolvenstraat 23; ⏰ 9am-1am Sun-Thu, 9am-3am Fri & Sat; 🚊 13/14/17 Westermarkt

This funky cafe with no sign out the front is a go-to for simple daytime refreshments (try the buttermilk-and-orange-juice combo – honestly it's delicious) and a cool bar scene at night, all to a soundtrack of Biz Markie and The Clash.

⭐ PLAY

⭐ COC AMSTERDAM *Gay & Lesbian*

☎ 626 30 87; www.cocamsterdam.nl, in Dutch; Rozenstraat 14; 🚊 13/14/17 Westermarkt

HQ of the national gay and lesbian organisation holds weekly parties and other get-togethers.

⭐ DECO SAUNA *Sauna*

☎ 623 82 15; Herengracht 115; admission €19.50; ⏰ noon-11pm Mon & Wed-Sat, 3-11pm Tue, 1-8pm Sun; 🚊 1/2/5/13/17 Nieuwezijds Kolk

Steam yourself in art deco splendour – this beautiful sauna is a wonderful way to warm up on a grey afternoon. Note that it's all-nude and unisex, even in the dressing rooms.

⭐ FELIX MERITIS *Arts Centre*

☎ 626 13 11; www.felixmeritis.nl, in Dutch; Keizersgracht 324; ⏰ box office 10am-5pm Mon-Sat; 🚊 13/14/17 Westermarkt; ♿

This wonderful arts and culture space, established in 1777, occasionally hosts experimental European theatre, along with innovative music, dance, and lectures and readings. The cafe here, with its huge open windows, is particularly great.

WORTH THE TRIP

Just to the north of the Jordaan, the Westelijke Eilanden (Western Islands) were origi-nally home to shipworks and the West India Trading Company warehouses. The district is a world unto itself, cut through with canals and linked with small drawbridges. It's home to artists' studios and foodie favourite **Marius** (☎ 422 78 80; Barentszstraat 243; dinner Tue-Sat; 3 Zoutkeetsgracht) — Chef Kees is an alumnus of California's Chez Panisse.

To the west of the islands, **Het Schip** (☎ 418 28 85; www.hetschip.nl; Spaarn-dammerplantsoen 140; adult/child/concession €5/2/2.75; 1-5pm Wed-Sun; 22 Zaanstraat) is one of the most fabulous housing projects you'll ever see. The pinnacle — almost literally: check out that tower! — of Amsterdam School style (see boxed text, p106), it now hosts a small museum in three parts: you can poke around the delightful old post office, walk through an apartment and enjoy a drink in the teahouse.

From Het Schip, you can walk back southeast along the train tracks and cut through a small underpass to Westerpark. This sprawling patch of green is a bit of a hipster hangout, perhaps because it's adjacent to **Westergasfabriek** (☎ 586 07 10; www .westergasfabriek.nl; Haarlemmerweg 8-10; 3 Haarlemmerplein), a former gasworks that has been transformed into an edgy cultural park, filled with bars, concert halls and restaurants.

⭐ MALOE MELO *Live Music*

☎ 420 45 92; Lijnbaansgracht 163;
🕙 9pm-3am Sun-Thu, 9pm-4am Fri &
Sat; 🚃 7/10/17 Elandsgracht

Home to Amsterdam's blues
scene, this dingy venue is rowdy
and casual, and often adds blue-
grass and soul to the calendar. If
nothing appeals here, goth and
new-wave **Korsakoff** (☎ 625 78 54;
Lijnbaansgracht 161), next door,
might do.

⭐ MOVIES *Cinema*

☎ 638 60 16; www.themovies.nl;
Haarlemmerdijk 157-165; adult/student/
child €8/7/6.50; 🕙 1.30pm-midnight;
🚃 3 Haarlemmerplein

Indie features (often in English)
rule at this beautiful art deco
cinema. The sweet Wild Kitchen
restaurant offers a reasonable
package of a two-course meal and
movie ticket for €28.

SOUTHERN CANAL BELT

>SOUTHERN CANAL BELT

The southern stretch of the Grachtengordel, completed when the city was wallowing in cash at the end of the 17th century, is even ritzier than the western area. Yet even the double-wide mansions on the so-called Gouden Bocht (Golden Bend) – the Herengracht between Leidsestraat and Vijzelstraat – are not gaudy: the various styles all blend into a seamless whole. The interiors of the lovely homes here are grand too – at least judging from the shops along Nieuwe Spiegelstraat, Amsterdam's address for museum-quality antiques.

At either end of the neighbourhood, old-money gives way to neon glitz in the Leidseplein and Rembrandtplein. Feeding into the Leidseplein is the shopping street of Leidsestraat, packed with a disproportionately large number of shoe shops and fast-food outlets. South of Rembrandtplein, the Utrechtsestraat is a chic strip of boutiques and excellent restaurants.

SOUTHERN CANAL BELT

Please see over for map

Bloomin' marvellous: the Bloemenmarkt is an Amsterdam icon

👁 SEE

◎ BLOEMENMARKT
Singel btwn Koningsplein & Muntplein; ⏲ **9am-5.30pm Mon-Sat, 11am-5.30pm Sun;** 🚋 **1/2/5 Koningsplein**
This canalside flower market has been here since the 1860s, when gardeners used to sail up the Amstel and sell from their boats. Many vendors sell more bulbs than cut flowers, so it's not the riot of colour you might have expected, but it's still a pretty place for a stroll, and perhaps to pick up a bouquet to brighten up your hotel room.

◎ DE APPEL
☎ **622 56 51; www.deappel.nl; Nieuwe Spiegelstraat 10; admission €7;** ⏲ **11am-6pm Tue-Sun;** 🚋 **16/24/25 Keizersgracht;** ♿
This cutting-edge contemporary art space holds adventurous but accessible exhibitions of conceptual art, which are grounded in theory while making connections with everyday life.

◎ FOAM
Fotografiemuseum Amsterdam; ☎ **551 65 00; www.foam.nl; Keizersgracht 609; admission €7/5;** ⏲ **10am-6pm Sat-Wed, 10am-9pm Thu & Fri;** 🚋 **16/24/25 Keizersgracht**
Rotating work at this hyper-modernised canal-house space ranges from that of photography giants such as Richard Avedon to relative unknowns like Malick Sidibé, a Malian portraitist. The museum also prints an edgy magazine four times a year and hosts a variety of photographers' confabs.

NEIGHBOURHOODS

SOUTHERN CANAL BELT

☺ HERMITAGE AMSTERDAM

☎ 530 87 55; www.hermitage.nl; Nieuwe Herengracht 14; admission €7/free; ⏱ 10am-5pm; 🚊 9/14 Waterlooplein

Given Peter the Great's admiration of Golden Age Amsterdam (the canals were the model for those in central St Petersburg), this satellite of the Russian Hermitage Museum makes perfect sense. By mid-2009 the main museum space should open in this, the vast Amstelhof, an old-age home since the 17th century; in the meantime, there's just a small selection of treasures in an adjacent house.

☺ MUSEUM VAN LOON

☎ 624 52 55; www.museumvanloon .nl; Keizersgracht 672; admission €6/4; ⏱ 11am-5pm Wed-Mon; 🚊 16/24/25 Keizersgracht

Arguably the best of the canal-house museums, this 1672 mansion was first home to painter Ferdinand Bol; in the 19th century, the Van Loon family (descendants of Willem van Loon, cofounder of the Dutch East India Company) moved in. Start in the basement with the introductory video, in which a family member tells anecdotes about visiting his grandmother in the house, then wander through the shadowy rooms adorned with rich wallpaper, worn carpets and well-used Louis XV furniture.

☺ MUSEUM WILLET-HOLTHUYSEN

☎ 523 18 22; www.willetholthuysen .nl; Herengracht 605; admission €5/2.50; ⏱ 10am-5pm Mon-Fri, 11am-5pm Sat & Sun; 🚊 4/9/14 Rembrandtplein

This mansion has been a museum since 1895, when a wealthy widow gave the city her home and her husband's assorted treasures – furniture, paintings and loads of 18th-century china. It's a bit fussier than the Van Loon (left), but the *objets* are lovely.

☺ REFLEX MODERN ART GALLERY

☎ 627 28 32; www.reflex-art.nl; Weteringschans 79a; admission free; ⏱ 11am-6pm Tue-Sat; 🚊 7/10 Spiegelgracht

Reflex is the city's biggest commercial gallery, dealing in works by Karel Appel, Willem de Kooning and Jeff Koons. Just across the intersection, at Weteringschans 83, a second space displays more contemporary work – look for David LaChapelle, Nobuyoshi Araki and others here.

☺ STADSARCHIEF

Municipal Archives; ☎ 251 15 11; www .stadsarchief.amsterdam.nl, in Dutch; Vijzelstraat 32; admission free, audio tour €4; ⏱ 10am-5pm Tue-Fri, 11am-5pm Sun; 🚊 16/24/25 Keizersgracht; ♿ The Amsterdam archives occupy a monumental bank building which dates from 1923. When you step inside head to the left, to the enormous tiled basement vault and displays of archive gems such as the 1942 police report on the theft of Anne Frank's bike. A small cinema at the back shows vintage films about the city. Upstairs, a gallery space is dedicated to temporary exhibits (for a small entry fee), and there's a good bookshop. Free tours of the building run at 1pm from Tuesday to Friday and at 3pm on Saturday and Sunday.

◔ TASSENMUSEUM HENDRIKJE
☎ 524 64 52; www.tassenmuseum.nl; Herengracht 573; admission €6.50/5; ◔ 10am-5pm; 🚊 4/9/14 Rembrandtplein
Dedicated entirely to handbags, this chic canal-house museum is surprisingly interesting even for nonfashionistas. However, the signage is not as thorough as it could be and, in what seems like a major gap, there's no Birkin on display.

◔ TUSCHINSKITHEATER
☎ 626 26 33; www.pathe.nl, in Dutch; Reguliersbreestraat 26; admission €9-10; ◔ noon-10pm; 🚊 4/9/14 Rembrandtplein
Built in 1921, this fantastic theatre melds art deco and Amsterdam School architecture. Faithfully restored, the interior features a huge

handmade carpet and a striking cupola that should never meet the gaze of someone on hallucinogens. You'll have to endure a Hollywood blockbuster to eyeball the marvellous main hall, but then you can also peek at the Japanese Room upstairs. While you're here, note the Cineac building across the street – this austere functionalist building was erected just over a decade later.

🛍 SHOP
🛍 BEBOB DESIGN Design
☎ 624 57 63; Prinsengracht 764; ◔ 11am-6pm & 7-9pm Thu,11am-6pm Fri-Sat; 🚊 4 Prinsengracht
Those with a midcentury-modern chair fetish will be sated with Eames, Aalto and others at this second-hand design warehouse. Shipping can be arranged, but a George Nelson ball clock should fit nicely in your carry-on.

🛍 CONCERTO Music
☎ 623 52 28; Utrechtsestraat 52-60; ◔ 10am-6pm Mon-Wed, Fri & Sat, 10am-9pm Thu, noon-6pm Sun; 🚊 4 Keizersgracht
Spread over several buildings, this is the city's most engaging music store. Ideal for browsing, it has an eclectic (and often cheap) collection of new and second-hand records, CDs and DVDs, and good listening facilities.

☐ CONSCIOUS DREAMS DREAMLOUNGE *Smart Shop*
☎ 626 69 07; www.consciousdreams.nl; Kerkstraat 113; ⏰ 11am-9pm Tue-Sat, noon-6pm Sun & Mon; 🚊 1/2/5 Prinsengracht

Amsterdam's original smart shop, founded in 1993, takes a holistic approach. It sells psychedelic mushrooms and trippy herbs (with educated recommendations from the staff), and also caters to the exhausted clubber with vitamin packs and other party-survival needs.

☐ CORA KEMPERMAN *Clothing*
☎ 625 12 84; Leidsestraat 72; 🚊 1/2/5 Prinsengracht

No matter what the season, Amsterdam's Cora Kemperman's striking, ethnic-inspired collections are defined by natural fabrics, crushed and crinkled looks, and lots of layers, volume and shape.

☐ EDUARD KRAMER *Antiques*
☎ 623 08 32; Nieuwe Spiegelstraat 64; 🚊 16/24/25 Keizersgracht

Specialising in antique Dutch tiles, this tiny store is also crammed with lots of other interesting stuff – silver candlesticks, crystal decanters, jewellery and pocket watches.

☐ FRED DE LA BRETONIÈRE *Footwear*
☎ 626 96 27; Utrechtsestraat 77; ⏰ 1-6pm Mon, 10am-6pm Tue, Wed & Fri, 10am-9pm Thu, 10am-5pm Sat, noon-5pm Sun; 🚊 4 Keizersgracht

A branch of the sensible-yet-fun Dutch shoe shop (p45).

☐ LAMBIEK *Books*
☎ 626 75 43; Kerkstraat 132; ⏰ 11am-6pm Mon-Fri, 11am-5pm Sat, 1-5pm Sun; 🚊 16/24/25 Keizersgracht

Comics specialist Lambiek has been in operation since 1968, stocking an impressive range of underground comics and newspaper strips, along with classics such as Tintin and Asterix. A gallery displays new comix-inspired art.

☐ TINKERBELL *Children's*
☎ 625 88 30; Spiegelgracht 10; ⏰ Mon-Sat; 🚊 7/10 Spiegelgracht

The mechanical bear that blows bubbles outside this shop fascinates kids; inside, there's a great selection of wood toys, historical costumes and plush animals – no blinking lights or batteries here.

☐ YOUNG DESIGNERS UNITED *Clothing*
☎ 626 91 91; Keizersgracht 447; ⏰ 1-6pm Mon, 10am-6pm Tue-Sat; 🚊 1/2/5 Keizersgracht

This boutique showcases young Dutch designers, each displayed on its own rack. The range is huge, from abstract, asymmetrical sheaths to sexy, flower-bedecked frocks, all fairly well priced.

Yasmina Aboutaleb
Culture critic for youth magazine CJP

Best buy Theatre tickets are inexpensive, and there's more and more subtitling and English. **What you'll see** Sometimes it seems like you can't go to a show without seeing a guy playing the piano – with his penis out. Directors call it 'functional' nudity. **Diversity onstage** Sometimes I'm the only curly-haired person in the theatre. To see people like me, I have to go out to the West, to someplace like Podium Mozaiëk (p75). But those people should all come to the centre! **Post-Theo** A few artists rallied for freedom of speech. Others called for more nudity – one director said: 'Boobs can't hurt – arms do!' **Post-show** Everyone goes to De Smoeshaan (p91) – but I prefer De Doelen (p130), an old-fashioned place where you can grab a pickled egg from the jar on the bar.

🍴 EAT

🍴 COFFEE & JAZZ *Indonesian* €
☎ 624 58 51; Utrechtsestraat 113;
🕑 11am-11pm Tue-Fri, 10am-4pm Sat;
🚊 4 Prinsengracht; Ⓥ

'Coffee & Jazz & Surprisingly Tasty Indonesian Food' isn't quite as catchy, but more accurate. This one-man operation is typical eccentric Amsterdam – a must for jazz freaks and anyone who loves a snug place with a passionate owner.

🍴 FEBO *Fast Food* €
☎ 620 86 15; Leidsestraat 94; 🕑 11am-3am Sun-Thu, 11am-4am Fri & Sat;
🚊 1/2/5 Prinsengracht; ♿ Ⓥ ♿

We don't exactly recommend this Dutch fast-food icon. The *bami* rolls are hot as napalm, the *frikadel* frightening and the *kaassoufflé* utterly unsoufflélike. But plucking a treat from the yellow automat windows is a drunken Dutch tradition. And the *frites* (from the counter) are pretty good, complete with sauce on the side. There's another near Rembrandtplein (Reguliersbreestraat 38), but for deep-fried goodness in that area, don't miss Van Dobben (p90).

🍴 LE ZINC...ET LES AUTRES
French €€
☎ 622 90 44; Prinsengracht 999;
🕑 5.30-11pm Tue-Sat;
🚊 4 Prinsengracht; Ⓥ

This cosy old canal-house restaurant is an unapologetically old-fashioned affair, as well as being quite a romantic address. The menu matches the vibe well – rustic dishes like pigeon and rabbit, with an option of matched wines alongside each course.

🍴 LOS PILONES *Mexican* €€
☎ 320 46 51; Kerkstraat 63; 🕑 4-11.30pm Tue-Sun; 🚊 1/2/5 Prinsengracht; Ⓥ ♿

Yes, this place has excellent Mexican food, cooked by Mexicans who know what dishes like *cochinita pibil* should taste like. But that's probably not why you came to Amsterdam; we recommend it more because it's a quality place that, with its colourful, casual fiesta atmosphere, is also child-friendly.

🍴 MAOZ *Fast Food* €
☎ 420 74 35; Muntplein 1; 🕑 11am-1am Sun-Thu, 11am-3pm Fri & Sat;
🚊 4/9/14/24/25 Muntplein; ♿ Ⓥ ♿

Falafel, saviour of vegetarians the world over, is perfected at this minichain, which has now expanded beyond the Netherlands. Just €4 gets you a falafel with unlimited access to a massive salad bar – a true test of your pita's strength. There's another outlet at Leidsestraat 85.

HOW TO EAT A HERRING

'Hollandse Nieuwe' isn't a fashion trend – it's the fresh catch of supertasty herring, raked in every June. The season's precise start date depends on when the little fish reach their prime fattiness, and it's greeted with all the fanfare that the new Beaujolais would be elsewhere. Although Dutch tradition calls for dangling the *haring* above your mouth, this isn't the way it's done in Amsterdam. Here the fish is served chopped in chunks, and eaten with a toothpick, topped with *uitjes* (chopped onions) and *zuur* (sweet pickles). A *broodje haring* is even handier, as the fluffy white roll holds on the toppings and keeps your fingers fish-fat-free – think of it as an edible napkin.

🍴 PATA NEGRA *Spanish* €€

☎ 422 62 50; Utrechtsestraat 142; 🕐 noon-midnight Sun-Thu, noon-1am Fri & Sat; 🚊 4 Prinsengracht

Pata Negra has been around since 1997, dishing up supergarlicky prawns, grilled sardines and other savoury treats. It can get impossibly crowded, especially on weekends – arrive before 6.30pm or reserve a table. The kitchen is open until 11pm (11.30pm on weekends).

🍴 SEGUGIO *Italian* €€€

☎ 330 15 03; Utrechtsestraat 96; 🕐 6-11pm Mon-Sat; 🚊 4 Prinsengracht; Ⓥ

This refined little Italian job on busy Utrechtsestraat is one of Amsterdam's best. Well-spaced tables and accomplished handling of first-rate ingredients (such as truffles and scallops) mark it as the perfect place for a romantic tête-à-tête, despite the fact that there are no candles on the tables (scandal!).

🍴 TEMPO DOELOE *Indonesian* €€

☎ 625 67 18; Utrechtsestraat 75; 🕐 6-11.30pm; 🚊 4 Keizersgracht; Ⓥ

One of the most respected Indonesian restaurants in the city, this tiny place is more formal than most. It's a good place for solo diners to try *rijsttafel* (a spiced rice dish; many places will do it only for two), though the à la carte options are arguably better. There's a nice wine list, and reservations are required.

🍴 TUJUH MARET *Indonesian* €€

☎ 427 98 65; www.tujuh-maret.com; Utrechtsestraat 73; 🕐 lunch Mon-Sat, dinner daily; 🚊 4 Keizersgracht; ♿ Ⓥ 🚻

The owners of Tempo Doeloe (above) also run this more casual spot next door. Grab a wicker chair and tuck into spicy dishes like dried, fried beef or chicken in red-pepper sauce. There's a *rijsttafel*, but the regular menu is preferable.

🍴 VAN DOBBEN
Sandwich Shop €

☎ 624 42 00; Korte Reguliersd-warsstraat 5; ⏲ 9.30am-1am Mon-Fri, 9.30am-2am Sat, 11.30am-8pm Sun; 🚊 4/9/14 Rembrandtplein

Open since the 1940s, the venerable Van Dobben has white tile walls, white-coated counter men who brusquely take your order, white glasses of milk next to fluffy white *broodje* rolls. The only colour comes from the meat – heaps of sliced roast beef glow like rubies, and your much-Dutcher-than-you neighbour is probably eating a glistening red plate of steak tartare. Try the *pekelvlees* (something resembling corned beef), or make it a *halfom*, if you're keen on that being mixed with liver.

🍴 WALEM *Cafe* €

☎ 625 35 44; Keizersgracht 449; ⏲ 10am-1am; 🚊 1/2/5 Keizersgracht

Two terraces, friendly service and a changing menu keep this grand cafe, which is run by the same team who do a solid job at De Jaren (p47), in the Centrum, popular. There's a line of soups and salads, as well as a few simple mains, but overall it's just a great place to chill out, regroup and appreciate the industrial-mod style of this great Gerrit Rietveld building.

🍴 WOK TO WALK *Chinese* €

☎ 624 29 41; Leidsestraat 96; ⏲ 9am-late; 🚊 1/2/5 Prinsengracht; ♿ 🅥

Many fast-food joints in Amsterdam assume you're too drunk or stoned to care what you're eating. Wok to Walk, however, serves fast food fresh. Choose noodles or rice, meat or veg, and a sauce; add to a wok and stir. There are other branches, but the culinary wasteland of Leidsestraat is where you'll need one most.

🍸 DRINK

🍸 BARNEY'S LOUNGE
Coffeeshop

☎ 420 66 55; Reguliersgracht 27; ⏲ 9am-1am; 🚊 4 Keizersgracht

A branch of the Haarlemmerdijk institution (p73), located on a beautiful and quiet stretch of canal.

🍸 CAFÉ AMERICAIN *Cafe*

☎ 556 32 32; Leidsekade 97; ⏲ 7am-10pm; 🚊 1/2/5/7/10 Leidseplein

The art deco interior of this grand cafe, with its vaulted ceiling and stained-glass windows, is one of Amsterdam's most stylish and easily justifies a drink or two here, if only to have a peek.

🍸 DE HUYSCHKAEMER *Bar*

☎ 627 05 75; Utrechtsestraat 137; 🚊 4 Prinsengracht

Of all the bars along Utrechtsestraat, this one attracts the most mixed crowd – gay and straight, expat and local, old and young – and it spills out onto the sidewalk on weekends. The setting is an old-fashioned split-level room, but the decor is modern, with sleek booths along the walls.

☕ DE KOFFIE SALON *Cafe*
☎ 330 43 14; Utrechtsestraat 130; ⏱ 7am-7pm; 🚋 4 Prinsengracht; Ⓥ ♿

Stay in and sip your coffee in this split-level lounge (there's a big couch section upstairs) or take it to go, a relative rarity in this city. The baristas are cheerful and friendly, and there are *stroopwafels* and other goodies from Lanskroon (p50).

☕ DE SMOESHAAN *Cafe*
☎ 625 03 68; Leidsekade 90; ⏱ 11am-1am, Sun-Thu, 11am-2am Fri & Sat; 🚋 1/2/5/7/10 Leidseplein

Theater Bellevue's cafe gets pretty lively before and after the shows, with theatre visitors and performers. During the day it's a nice place to relax within view of the Singelgracht. The pub food is better than it needs to be – try the *gehakt* (meatloaf) at lunch time.

☕ HEUVEL *Brown Cafe*
☎ 622 63 54; Prinsengracht 568; 🚋 7/10 Spiegelgracht

If you're footsore from antiques shopping in the neighbourhood, stop in at this equally antique cafe, a local favourite for its position on a busy corner.

☕ ROKERIJ *Coffeeshop*
☎ 422 66 43; Lange Leidsedwarsstraat 41; ⏱ 10am-1am Mon-Thu & Sun, 10am-3am Fri & Sat; 🚋 1/2/5 Prinsengracht

Behind the black hole of an entrance you'll find Asian decor and candlelight for those tired of the Rastafarian vibe. There's another, tiny branch at Amstel 8.

☕ SCHILLER *Cafe*
☎ 624 98 46; Rembrandtplein 26; 🚋 4/9/14 Rembrandtplein

With a fabulous art deco interior, this is the sole piece of old-fashioned charm on the raucous Rembrandtplein. Walls are lined with portraits of long-dead Dutch actors and cabaret artists, and tippling journalists often occupy the bar stools and booths.

☕ VIVELAVIE *Gay & Lesbian*
☎ 624 01 14; Amstelstraat 7; ⏱ 3pm-1am Sun-Thu, 3pm-3am Fri & Sat; 🚋 4/9/14 Rembrandtplein

Amsterdam's most popular lesbian bar has friendly bar staff, great music, and a lovely summer terrace. It's a great place for a late-night drink.

☿ WEBER *Lounge*
☎ 627 05 74; Marnixstraat 397;
🕐 8pm-3am Mon-Thu, 8pm-4am Fri-Sun; 🚊 1/2/5/7/10 Leidseplein

A great buzzy bar with loud indie music and a less pretentious vibe than the overtly hip decor might suggest. The only catch is that it's impossibly small, but the owners solved that by opening neighbouring Kamer 401 (No 401) and Lux (No 403); the latter is practically a mirror image of Weber – confusing after a couple of drinks.

★ PLAY

▣ BOOM CHICAGO *Comedy*
☎ 423 01 01; www.boomchicago.nl; Leidseplein 12; admission €10-22; 🕐 box office 11.30am-8.30pm; 🚊 1/2/5/7/10 Leidseplein; ♿

This hilarious English-language improv troupe has been playing to enthusiastic crowds since 1993, and its members have gone on to *Saturday Night Live*, *The Colbert Report* and other American comedy mainstays. The topical shows riff on local and European issues – it's a surprisingly good place to get the pulse of Amsterdam politics.

▣ ESCAPE *Nightclub*
☎ 622 11 11; www.escape.nl; Rembrandtplein 11; 🕐 11pm-4am Thu, 11pm-5am Fri & Sat, 11pm-4.30am Sun; 🚊 4/9/14 Rembrandtplein; ♿

Amsterdam's biggest, glitziest club has managed to keep the

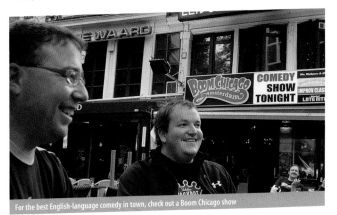

For the best English-language comedy in town, check out a Boom Chicago show bass pumping since the '80s; it got a major tech revamp in 2007. Except for the once-a-month gay night, the scene can be pretty generic, with a long line at the door to boot – we recommend it only if there's a well-known DJ at the helm.

☆ JAZZ CAFÉ ALTO *Live Music*
☎ 626 32 49; Korte Leidsedwarsstraat 115; admission free; 🕙 9pm-3am Sun-Thu, 9pm-4am Fri & Sat; 🚋 7/10 Spiegelgracht

Smack in Amsterdam's touristy heart is this renowned gem of a jazz club – it's so small that you feel as though you're part of the musical conversation between the band members. Admittedly, drinks are a little pricey (to make up for the free admission), but not outrageous.

GET *UIT* AND ABOUT
Not sure how to spend your evening? Head to the last-minute ticket desk at the Uitburo (☎ 621 13 11; www .aub.nl; 🕙 10am-7.30pm Mon-Sat, noon-7.30pm Sun), in the corner of the Stadsschouwburg on the Leidseplein. Comedy, dance, concerts, even club nights are all potentially available at a significant discount – and handily marked 'LNP' (language no problem) if the event doesn't hinge on understanding Dutch to have fun.

☆ JIMMY WOO *Nightclub*
☎ 626 31 50; www.jimmywoo.com; Korte Leidsedwarsstraat 18; 🕙 11pm-3am Wed, Thu & Sun, 11pm-4am Fri & Sat; 🚋 1/2/5/7/10 Leidseplein

Opium-den decor and a very serious door policy keep the intimate domain of Jimmy Woo at the top of the cool list, at least among Amsterdam's rich and beautiful. If you're up for it, dress glam, be sweet to the door staff and get on a list if you can, perhaps through your hotel.

☆ MELKWEG *Arts Centre*
☎ 531 81 81; www.melkweg.nl; Lijnbaansgracht 234a; 🚋 1/2/5/7/10 Leidseplein; ♿

The Milky Way – it's housed in a former dairy – must be Amsterdam's coolest club-gallery-cinema-cafe-concert hall. Its vibrant program of events is so full and varied that it's impossible not to find something you want to go to, from international DJ club nights to live Brazilian jazz.

☆ ODEON *Nightclub*
☎ 521 85 55; www.odeontheater .nl; Singel 460; 🕙 Thu-Sat; 🚋 1/2/5 Koningsplein

Set in a skinny canal house, the Odeon has been a creative party spot for decades. A 2005 makeover made it a bit more glam, but it's still accessible, with a separate

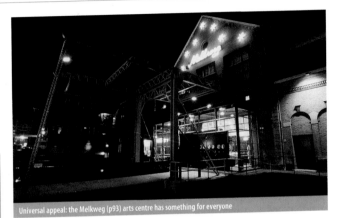

Universal appeal: the Melkweg (p93) arts centre has something for everyone

cocktail bar and cafe, and its club nights cater to a crowd that's been partying since the '80s. Entry is rarely more than €15.

⭐ PARADISO
Nightclub, Live Music

☎ 626 45 21; www.paradiso.nl; Weteringschans 6-8; 🕒 Fri-Sun 11.30pm-4am; 🚃 7/10 Spiegelgracht; ♿

Amsterdam's best live-music venue, set in a former church, attracts big names despite its relatively small size. When the bands finish, the space becomes an excellent, no-pretensions club. Expect interesting dance music, anything from Finnish DJs spinning jazz to Afro New Wave from New York and tech-hop from Detroit. Admission varies according to the night,

and generally ranges from free to €25.

⭐ STADSSCHOUWBURG
Concert Hall, Theatre

☎ 624 23 11; www.ssba.nl, in Dutch; Leidseplein 26; tickets €12-80; 🕒 box office 10am-6pm; 🚃 1/2/5/7/10 Leidseplein; ♿

This beautiful baroque building is the city's most impressive theatre, hosting large-scale touring productions, dance and drama by Toneelgroep Amsterdam.

⭐ STUDIO 80 *Nightclub*

☎ 521 83 33; www.studio-80.nl; Rembrandtplein 17; 🚃 4/9/14 Rembrandtplein

It's all about the (electronic) music at this raw space, which functions as much as a studio and radio station as a club. It hosts parties several nights a week – the M.U.L.T.I.S.E.X.I. bash is one of the most popular. Cheap entry guarantees a young crowd.

⭐ SUGAR FACTORY
Live Music, Nightclub
☎ 626 50 06; www.sugarfactory.nl; Lijnbaansgracht 238; ⏱ 6.30pm-1am

Mon-Thu, 6.30pm-2am Fri & Sat, 7pm-1am Sun; 🚊 1/2/5/7/10 Leidseplein
One night it's Balkan beats; another, it's a 10-piece soul band – the Sugar Factory has all kinds of live entertainment. Equally important, the vibe is always welcoming and creative. It's an excellent midsize space, with a smoking lounge upstairs. Check the website to see if your first name's on the monthly list for free entry!

>VONDELPARK & OLD SOUTH

Canny Amsterdammers financed Vondelpark in the 1860s by reclaiming more land than necessary, then selling the excess to developers on the condition that no factories or workers' cottages be built. Thus arose Oud Zuid (Old South), one of Amsterdam's most gracious neighbourhoods, and one of its wealthiest. The tree-shaded old homes along the park are a beautiful area to wander aimlessly – the houses get bigger the further south you go.

Adjacent to all this are the city's best art collections. The Rijksmuseum (p98) is the granddaddy, a 1885 Dutch Renaissance–style behemoth by PJH Cuypers, who also designed Centraal Station. When it and the nearby Concertgebouw (1888) were built, the area between them was still farmland. Now it's a big patch of grass called Museumplein, handy for footsore tourists and well used by locals too, especially in winter, when an ice-skating rink is installed. There's a cafe on the north side (check out the toilets!), a skate ramp and the highly photogenic 'I amsterdam' sign.

VONDELPARK & OLD SOUTH

⦿ SEE

◉ RIJKSMUSEUM

☎ 674 70 00; www.rijksmuseum.nl; Jan Luijkenstraat 1; adult/child under 18yr €10/free; ☷ 9am-6pm Sat-Thu, 9am-8.30pm Fri; 🚊 2/5 Hobbemastraat; ♿
The city's main art attraction can get mobbed, so it helps to buy tickets online and bypass the queue. A leisurely stroll through the 'greatest hits' collection takes about two hours. Also poke around in the museum's gardens (free), which are dotted with sculpture and pieces of architectural detail.

◉ STEDELIJK MUSEUM

www.stedelijk.nl; Paulus Potterstraat 13; 🚊 2/3/5/12 Van Baerlestraat
Amsterdam's cutting-edge contemporary art collection is closed until early 2010 for renovations, which include adding an entrance that locals have dubbed 'the Bathtub'.

◉ VAN GOGH MUSEUM

☎ 570 52 00; www.vangoghmuseum.nl; Paulus Potterstraat 7; adult/child under 12yr/child 13-17yr €12/free/2.50, audio tour €4; ☷ 10am-6pm Sat-Thu, 10am-10pm Fri; 🚊 2/3/5/12 Van Baerlestraat; ♿

Spend some quality time with Vincent at the impressive Van Gogh Museum

FRIDAY NIGHT SKATE

This weekly event (www.fridaynightskate.com) is a great way to see the city. You'll also get to meet new people: hundreds of in-line skaters (perhaps thousands in peak season) gather at 8pm near the Filmmuseum in Vondelpark for departure at 8.30pm. The route varies each week, but generally it's a challenging 15km or 20km – you should be an experienced skater to participate. The event is cancelled if streets are wet, meaning that on average it actually takes place about twice a month. Rent skates at **De Vondeltuin** (☎ 062 756 55 76; www .vondeltuin.nl, in Dutch; Vondelpark 7; skate rental per hr/2hr/3hr adult €5/7.50/10; Mar-Oct), at the south end of the park.

The artist's sunflowers draw flocks of visitors to the Van Gogh Museum, so as with other major museums in town, it's possible to buy tickets online and skip the queue. Perhaps even more appealing is a visit on a Friday night, when it hosts some kind of live music and there's a party atmosphere. Until the Stedelijk Museum (opposite) reopens, the back wing here will mount a few temporary shows of its neighbour's collection.

⬤ VONDELPARK
Stadhouderskade; ⏱ 24hr; 🚊 2/5 **Hobbemastraat**
Enjoying Vondelpark is as simple as picking out your own patch of grass. But if you want a proper chair, head to **Vertigo** (☎ 612 30 21), the cafe at the Filmmuseum (p103), near the park's main entrance. It serves solid food (try the *uitsmijter Vertigo,* an egg sandwich with mushrooms) and cold beer. In the centre of the park, **'t Blauwe Theehuis** (☎ 662 02 54; ⏱ 9am-10pm) is a cafe inside what looks like a flying saucer – most people sit outside in the 700 or so terrace seats. Parents can let their kids roam at **Het Groot Melkhuis** (☎ 612 96 74; ⏱ 10am-dusk; ♿), a self-service cafe adjacent to a huge playground. Finally, the **Openluchttheater** (☎ 428 33 60; www .openluchttheater.nl) is an outdoor stage with a summer calendar of drama, live jazz, kids' shows and more, with completely free admission.

🛍 SHOP

🛍 & KLEVERING *Housewares*
☎ 670 36 23; Jacob Obrechtstraat 19a; 🚊 2 Jacob Obrechtstraat
If it's quirky, colourful and sits on your table, it's sure to be in this fun home-accessories shop. This is the place to pick up a great example of Dutch-designed cleverness without blowing your budget.

COSTER DIAMONDS
Jewellery

☎ 305 55 55; Paulus Potterstraat 2-6;
🕓 9am-5pm; 🚋 2/5 Hobbemastraat
Founded in 1840, Coster is famous
for having cut the Persian Koh-
I-Noor diamond in 1852. It's one
of Amsterdam's oldest diamond
factories still in operation, and one
you can trust.

FRED DE LA BRETONIÈRE
Footwear

☎ 470 93 20; Van Baerlestraat 34;
🕓 1-6pm Mon, 10am-6pm Tue, Wed &
Fri, 10am-9pm Thu, 10am-5pm Sat, noon-
5pm Sun; 🚋 2/3/5/12 Van Baerlestraat
A branch of the sensible-yet-fun
Dutch shoe shop (p45).

MARLIES DEKKERS *Clothing*

☎ 471 41 46; Cornelis Schuytstraat 13;
🕓 Mon-Sat; 🚋 2 Cornelis Schuytstraat
With a fireplace and chandeliers,
and bonbons to nibble, this shop
is the perfect setting for the gorgeous, racy work of Dutch lingerie
designer Dekkers (her 'bare butt
dress' is ensconced in a Rotterdam
design museum).

OILILY *Clothing, Children's*

☎ 672 33 61; Pieter Cornelisz
Hooftstraat 131-133; 🚋 2/3/5/12 Van
Baerlestraat
The sturdy, psychedelically pat-
terned cottons at this high-end
chain look good on kids, and on
their cool mums. Just be careful
you don't wind up with an actual
mother-daughter outfit.

PAUW *Clothing*

☎ 662 62 53; Van Baerlestraat 72;
🚋 2/3/5/12 Van Baerlestraat
Pauw means 'peacock', but the
clothes at this elegant Dutch
minichain are more formal than
flashy, with taffeta in gemlike
shades, equestrian-style coats
and sculptural blouses. There's
a men's shop down the road at
No 90, and another women's
boutique at No 66.

PIED À TERRE *Books*

☎ 627 44 55; Overtoom 135-137;
🕓 Mon-Sat; 🚋 1 1e Constantijn
Huygensstraat
With galleries and a skylight,
this travel-book shop feels like a
Renaissance centre of learning. It
stocks hiking and cycling tomes,
topographical maps and assorted
travel guides, including many in
English.

🍴 EAT

DE BAKKERSWINKEL
Cafe, Bakery   €

☎ 662 35 94; Roelof Hartstraat 68;
🕓 7am-4pm Tue-Sat, 10am-4pm Sun;
🚋 3/5/12/24 Roelof Hartplein; Ⓥ 🚻
A branch of the Warmoesstraat
bakery (p47).

☯ DE PEPER *Vegetarian* €
☎ 412 29 54; www.depeper.org;
Overtoom 301; ☯ 6-8.30pm Tue, Fri &
Sun; ☯ 1 Jan Pieter Heijestraat
The friendly restaurant at the
OT301 squat (p103) serves cheap
organic vegan meals – a great
place to connect with likeminded folks. Same-day
reservations are required.

☯ LA FALOTE *Dutch* €
☎ 622 54 54; Roelof Hartstraat 26;
☯ dinner Mon-Sat; ☯ 3/5/12/24
Roelof Hartplein; ☯ ☯
Echt Nederlands home-style
cooking such as calf's liver or
meatballs with endives. With
a daily special coming in at
under €10, this is a bargain in an
otherwise ritzy neighbourhood.
Wait till the owner brings out the
accordion.

☯ LOETJE *Dutch* €€
☎ 662 81 73; Johannes Vermeerstraat
52; ☯ lunch Mon-Fri, dinner Mon-Sat;
☯ 16/24 Ruysdaelstraat; ☯
This cafe's short menu may be
written on the chalkboard, but
everyone just orders thick steak,
served medium-rare and
swimming in delicious brown
gravy. The staff are surprisingly
good humoured, particularly
considering the loud, meat-
drunken mobs they typically
serve!

☯ OVERTOOM GROENTE EN
FRUIT *Turkish* €
☎ 683 98 88; Overtoom 129; ☯ 9am-
6pm; ☯ 1 1e Constantijn Huygensstraat
This Turkish grocery has a range
of premade salads and snacks,
perfect for picnics in the park.

☯ PALOMA BLANCA
Moroccan €€
☎ 612 64 85; Jan Pieter Heijestraat
145; ☯ dinner Tue-Sun; ☯ 1 Jan Pieter
Heijestraat; ☑ ☯
The name is Spanish, but the
lanterns, dishware and mosaic-top
tables are straight out of Mar-
rakech. Start off with *brik* (spicy
tuna spread) or stuffed squid; for a
main, get a rich, buttery couscous.
No alcohol.

☯ DRINK

☯ DE KOFFIE SALON *Cafe*
☎ 612 40 79; 1e Constantijn
Huygensstraat 82; ☯ 7am-7pm;
☯ 3/12 Overtoom; ☑
A branch of the excellent coffee
bar on the Utrechtsestraat (p91).

☯ HOLLANDSCHE MANEGE
Cafe
☎ 618 09 42; Vondelstraat 140;
☯ 2-11pm Mon-Thu, 9am-11pm Wed,
9am-6pm Sat, 9am-5pm Sun; ☯ 1 1e
Constantijn Huygensstraat; ☯
The elegant cafe at this riding
school, built in 1882, is one of the

city's greatest treasures. It overlooks the large arena, softly sunlit and smelling of hay and horses. To get there, enter through the long arcade on Vondelstraat, turn left and head up the stairs.

☰ WELLING *Brown Cafe*
☎ 662 01 55; Jan Willem Brouwersstraat 32; ⏱ 4pm-1am Mon-Fri, 3pm-1am Sat & Sun; 🚊 3/5/12/16/24 Museumplein
Behind the Concertgebouw, this local bar feels more like a library – but one where you're allowed to drink beer and have loud philosophical arguments. Regulars include notable artists and intellectuals, and an excellent cat.

☰ WILDSCHUT *Cafe*
☎ 676 82 20; Roelof Hartplein 1; 🚊 3/5/12/24 Roelof Hartplein; ♿
In warm weather, join the crowd on the front terrace with a view of Amsterdam School buildings (see boxed text, p106) or, when skies are grey, marvel at the art deco interior. If you're fussy about such things, avoid the orange juice – last we checked it wasn't freshly squeezed.

★ PLAY

☆ CONCERTGEBOUW
Concert Hall
☎ 573 05 11, 671 83 45; www .concertgebouw.nl; Concertgebouwplein 2-6; ⏱ box office 10am-8.15pm; 🚊 3/5/12/16/24 Museumplein; ♿
Bernard Haitink, celebrated conductor of the Royal Concertgebouw Orchestra, once remarked that this world-famous hall – built in 1888 with near-perfect acoustics – was the orchestra's best instrument. In addition to evening performances, there are free short concerts every Wednesday at 12.30pm from September until the end of June. Those aged 27 or younger can queue for €7.50 tickets, available 45 minutes before each show.

Chill: Vondelpark is just the tonic for sore heads

⭐ FILMMUSEUM *Cinema*
☎ 589 14 00; www.filmmuseum.nl; Vondelpark 3; admission €7.80/5; 🚊 1 1e Constantijn Huygensstraat
The museum owns more than 40,000 films and screens everything from silent classics to contemporary Iranian art house in its Vondelpark pavilion or, during summer, outdoors on the terrace. In late 2010, the Filmmuseum will move to a dramatic new building in Amsterdam-Noord – check the website for details.

⭐ OT301 *Arts Centre*
www.squat.net/overtoom301; Overtoom 301; 🚊 1 Jan Pieter Heijestraat
This long-established squat in the former Netherlands Film Academy hosts an eclectic roster of bands and DJs, with an emphasis on the strange and fringey. It also screens obscure films on Tuesdays.

>DE PIJP

With its narrow streets crowded by a mix of people from all classes and countries, De Pijp is often called the Latin Quarter of Amsterdam. It's come a long way since the 19th century, when it was the city's first move towards unsupervised development. It was also its last, given the dismal results: some of its shoddy tenement blocks collapsed even as they were being built. But the cheap housing harboured artists and intellectuals from early on, and in the 1960s and '70s the government began refurbishing the tenement blocks for immigrants from Morocco, Turkey, Suriname and the Netherlands Antilles.

Since the 1990s, the area has become very desirable for young couples, as well as a sizeable gay population. The numerous cafes, restaurants and bars here have a bohemian feel (even when they're clearly catering to wealthier new Pijp residents). So does lush Sarphatipark, named for a tireless 19th-century philanthropist, Samuel Sarphati, who fought to improve health and housing conditions here. How pleased he'd be to see the place now!

DE PIJP

◑ SEE
◑ DE DAGERAAD

Lutmastraat; 🚊 **12/25 Cornelis Troostplein;** ♿
One of the best Amsterdam School housing projects aside from Het Schip (p78), 'The Dawn' is worth a visit if you're an architecture buff. The central structure, on PL Takstraat, is a dramatic curving staircase.

◑ HEINEKEN EXPERIENCE
☎ **523 94 36; www.heinekenexperience .com; Stadhouderskade 78; admission €15;** 🚊 **16/24 Stadhouderskade;** ♿
When we passed through, the renovation of the Heineken brewery-turned-museum was still underway, ahead of its reopening in November 2008. We suppose there will be more coloured lights, but the most important thing – the beer – will still be there at the end of the tour.

⬒ SHOP
⬒ ALBERT CUYPMARKT
Clothing, Food

Albert Cuypstraat btwn Van Woustraat & Ferdinand Bolstraat; ⏲ **10am-5pm Mon-Sat;** 🚊 **16/24 Albert Cuypstraat**
When you're cruising this vast general market, note the shops behind the stalls as well – there's neat fabric, cool clothing and shops like De Peperbol, at No 150, which sells bulk spices, kitchen gadgets, essential oils, even Dutch lollies and *zoethout* (liquorice root, good for chewing). Volksrijwielhandel Tornado, at No 214 has high-quality bike accessories. For more on the market, see p19.

⬒ APPEL 67 *Clothing*
☎ **676 14 54; 2e Jacob van Campenstraat 1;** ⏲ **11am-7pm Mon-Fri, 10am-6pm Sat;** 🚊 **16/24 Stadhouderskade**
If Amsterdam is the closest you'll get to Scandinavia on this trip,

BACK TO SCHOOL
When Amsterdam School architecture started around WWI, it was as much a political movement as an aesthetic one. Architects such as Pieter Kramer and Michel de Klerk were reacting to the decadent, elitist style of neo-Renaissance buildings like Centraal Station, but also to appalling housing conditions for the poor. Their fantastical public-funded housing projects resemble shells, waves and other organic forms; they were obsessive about details, designing everything down to the house numbers. Some details were a bit paternalistic and controlling – windows high in the wall were meant to deter leaning out and gossiping with neighbours – but in general the buildings were vast improvements. Stroll around De Dageraad (above), then visit the museum at Het Schip (p78).

Yalçın Cihangir and Dave Deutsch

Owners of De Fietsfabriek (p108), whose cargo bike is a Dutch design icon

Our goal Our Bakfiets is like a little car, for carrying kids and groceries. We want to create the Ferrari of bicycles. **Customise** With our *freak me fiets* ('pimp my ride') options, people say we changed the scenery on the street, which is a great compliment. Plus, putting your name or motto on a bike is a huge deterrent to theft. **Two-wheeled trip** Most people don't know about the little villages up in the Noord (p144). Go on a Sunday, and just bike from terrace to terrace and drink coffee. **No bike required** Wake up early, like 4 or 5am, or stay up late – but don't be drunk or stoned! – and walk around the canals. **Souvenir of Amsterdam** We hope people will learn something about biking here, and take that back to their own country. With the environment, and people getting fatter, biking *is* the future!

stop in to this boutique for Cheap Monday jeans, Mads Nørgaard knit dresses and plenty more, for both men and women.

DE EMAILLEKEIZER
Housewares

☎ 664 18 47; 1e Sweelinckstraat 15; ☾ Mon-Sat; ☒ 4/25 Stadhouderskade

Enamel is the stock in trade of this funky shop, which mixes traditional Dutch house numbers, advertising plaques and coffee tins with metal plates and teapots from Poland, Ghana and beyond. You can also nab African trade beads and Fela Kuti albums.

DE FIETSFABRIEK *Bicycles*

☎ 672 18 34; 1e Jacob van Campenstraat 12; ☾ Tue-Sun; ☒ 16/24 Stadhouderskade

De Fietsfabriek's signature 'box bike' is Amsterdam's equivalent of the double-wide stroller. The creative company has other clever models too, plus fantastic accessories. Custom orders – with your name and favourite colour, for example – take four weeks from the factory in Turkey. One of the owners also applies his creativity to cool streetwear, sold at YC Clothing, which is just down the street at No 27.

Leg it to the Albert Cuypmarkt (p106) for some great bargains on food and clothing

EAT

BAZAR *Turkish*   €
☎ 675 05 44; Albert Cuypstraat 182;
🕑 11am-1am Mon-Thu, 11am-2am
Fri, 9am-2am Sat, 9am-midnight Sun;
🚊 16/24 Albert Cuypstraat; Ⓥ ♿
Our 4-year-old critic dubbed
this hip Mid East cafe 'the most
beautiful restaurant in the world'.
With plenty of room and tolerant
staff, the place is great for younger
ones, and parents will like the variety of the food. The Turkish-style
breakfast (€8) is particularly nice.
Look for the golden angel atop
the building.

BURGERMEESTER
International   €
☎ 670 93 39; Albert Cuypstraat 48;
🕑 noon-11pm; 🚊 16/24 Albert
Cuypstraat; Ⓥ ♿
This sleek little bistro aims to be
the *burgemeester* (mayor) of meat,
and hits the mark. It uses only organic beef (or lamb, falafel or fish),
with toppings like spicy veggies,
bean sprouts, piri-piri mayo and
more. One strange fault: no *frites*.

DE TAART VAN M'N TANTE
Bakery & Sweets   €
☎ 776 46 00; Ferdinand Bolstraat 10;
🕑 10am-6pm; 🚊 16/24 Stadhouderskade; ♿ Ⓥ ♿
Entering this bright-pink, Barbie-
bedecked cake shop, keep an eye

out for children running off their
sugar rush. Once you set eyes on
the famous cakes (the designers do
wedding creations too), you probably won't notice anything else.

DE WAAGHALS
Vegetarian   €€
☎ 679 96 09; Frans Halsstraat 29;
🕑 5-9.30pm Tue-Sun; 🚊 16/24
Stadhouderskade; Ⓥ
The white-walled 'Dare-Devil' is
stylish enough that even non-
veggies might re-examine their
dining priorities. The menu concen-
trates on one country each month,
plus a few staples, such as a rich,
mushroom-heavy aubergine *daube*.

DE WITTE UYL
International   €€
☎ 670 04 58; Frans Halsstraat 26;
🕑 6pm-1am Tue-Sat; 🚊 16/24
Stadhouderskade; Ⓥ
No wonder this neighbourhood
fave is frequently packed: it uses
organic and free-range meat,
vegetarians aren't forgotten, and
there's a good by-the-glass wine
selection. The food ranges from
Japanese flavours to Italian.

GAZIANTEP/HARISON'S
Turkish   €
☎ 618 22 55; Van Woustraat 32; 🕑 8am-
5pm; 🚊 4/25 Stadhouderskade; Ⓥ ♿
The window says Bosnian, but
this corner bakery's stock is purely

Turkish, with excellent *lahmacun* (what the Dutch call 'Turkish pizza'), as well as breakfast cookies, savoury pies and big, chewy loaves of bread. Wash it down with some *ayran* (salty yogurt drink).

🍴 IJSCUYPJE
Bakery & Sweets   €

1e van der Helststraat 27; ⏰ **11am-11pm Mon-Sat, 1pm-11pm Sun;** 🚊 **16/24 Albert Cuypstraat;** ♿ **Ⓥ 🚻**
Superintense raspberry and rich chocolate make a fantastic combo at this excellent ice-cream stand just off the Albert Cuypmarkt.

🍴 KISMET *Turkish*   €
☎ **671 47 68; Albert Cuypstraat 64;** ⏰ **10am-10pm;** 🚊 **16/24 Albert Cuypstraat; Ⓥ 🚻**
Primarily a takeout joint, Kismet also has a couple of tables wedged in the back. Either way, it provides good, fresh-tasting Turkish staples such as stuffed eggplant, baked lamb and assorted salads.

🍴 LE HOLLANDAIS
French   €€€
☎ **679 12 48; Amsteldijk 41;** ⏰ **6.30-10.30pm Mon-Sat;** 🚊 **3 Amsteldijk**
This subdued split-level restaurant doesn't look like much, but it's helmed by a smart, thoughtful chef with a passion for regional

French food. The kitchen makes its own sausages and doesn't shy away from 'variety meats'; sweetbreads and black pudding abound!

🍴 MAOZ
Fast Food   €
☎ **664 80 64; Ferdinand Bolstraat 67; 11am-1am;** 🚊 **16/24 Albert Cuypstraat;** ♿ **Ⓥ 🚻**
A branch of the falafel operation (p88); there's another at 1e van de Helstraat 43.

🍴 OP DE TUIN
Mediterranean   €€
☎ **675 26 20; Karel du Jardinstraat 47;** ⏰ **4-10.30pm;** 🚊 **3/25 2e Van der Helststraat; Ⓥ 🚻**
This is the kind of informal neighbourhood restaurant where you can sit snacking on an antipasti platter (let the chef decide a mix of Mediterranean standards) or a light pasta dish, and fantasise that you live across the street. Many of the regulars do.

🍴 RUNNEBOOM
Bakery & Sweets   €
☎ **673 59 41; 1e van der Helststraat 49;** ⏰ **7am-5pm Mon, Wed & Fri, 7am-4pm Tue, Thu & Sat;** 🚊 **16/24 Albert Cuypstraat;** ♿ **Ⓥ 🚻**
Look for Bert and Ernie on the sign of this proletarian bakery. The best treat is a 'Runnie', a

currant bun filled with cream and cinnamon sugar.

🍴 TJING TJING *South African* €€

☎ 676 09 23; Cornelis Troostraat 56-58; ⏰ 2pm-late; 🚊 12/25 Cornelis Troostplein; ♿

You can sample ostrich, springbok and kudu here, but these exotics are secondary to the Cape Malay *bobotie*, a South African shepherd's pie – cooked with passion by the owner. On Sundays during summer, there's an all-you-can-eat *braai* (barbecue).

🍸 DRINK

🍸 GOLLEM *Beer Bar*

☎ 676 71 17; Daniel Stalpertstraat 74; 🚊 16/24 Albert Cuypstraat

A roomier branch of the Belgian specialist in the Centrum (p54).

🍸 GREENHOUSE *Coffeeshop*

☎ 673 74 30; Tolstraat 91; ⏰ 9am-1am Sun-Thu, 9am-2am Fri & Sat; 🚊 4 Lutmastraat

The mosaic-trimmed Greenhouse, in an out-of-the-way spot, is spacious and attracts a mostly local crowd. There's a nominal 'membership' process, to keep the rowdies out, but tourists are usually waved through; guys must be 25-plus.

🍸 KINGFISHER *Bar*

☎ 671 23 95; Ferdinand Bolstraat 24; ⏰ 11am-1am Mon-Thu, 11am-3am Fri & Sat; 🚊 16/24 Stadhouderskade

Kingfisher's casual brand of cool and laid-back bar staff ensure it's always busy. It's a lot of locals' 'local', and as it's on one of the main streets through De Pijp, it offers great people-watching both inside and out (creative bicyclists are just the start).

🍸 PILSVOGEL *Brown Cafe*

☎ 664 64 83; Gerard Douplein 14; ⏰ 10am-1am; 🚊 16/24 Albert Cuypstraat

The kitchen dispenses small plates and daily set meals to a 20-something crowd, but that's really secondary when you're sitting on De Pijp's loveliest, busiest corner. Watch the world go by, or at least its ambassadors.

⭐ PLAY

✚ DE BADCUYP *Arts Centre*

☎ 675 96 69; www.badcuyp.nl; 1e Sweelinckstraat 10; 🚊 4/25 Stadhouderskade; ♿

A very cool venue off the Albert Cuypmarkt, De Badcuyp reflects the multicultural neighbourhood, with African dance parties, salsa nights and touring artists from all over the world.

>OOSTERPARK & AROUND

The acclaimed Tropenmuseum (opposite), a collection of global ephemera, is a fitting gateway to the quiet neighbourhood Oosterpark, one of the city's most culturally diverse neighbourhoods. Unlike De Pijp (p104), Oosterpark has seen only the tiniest bit of gentrification and it's not (yet) on any trend-watchers' radar – this is precisely what makes it interesting.

A walk east from the museum down Eerste van Swindenstraat leads to the street market on Dapperstraat (opposite) and eventually into Javastraat, where old Dutch fish shops and working-class bars sit adjacent to Moroccan, Indian and Turkish groceries, and you'll occasionally spot people 'walking' their birds (in cages), a Surinamese custom. South of Javastraat is considered a so-called 'dish city' – a stretch of apartment blocks studded with satellite dishes which, since the heated immigration debates of 2002, have become the symbols of what many Dutch consider to be 'unassimilated' foreigners.

After a cheap and tasty lunch the best place to relax is the district's namesake, Oosterpark, a lush patch of English-style landscaping that dates from the 1880s.

OOSTERPARK & AROUND

Please see over for map

SEE

OOSTERPARK

's-Gravesandestraat; 🕑 dawn-dusk; 🚊 3/7 Beukenweg

Oosterpark was laid out in 1891 to accommodate the *nouveaux-riches* diamond traders who found their fortunes in the South African mines, and it still has an elegant, rambling feel. On the south side, look for two monuments: one commemorates the abolition of slavery in the Netherlands in 1819, and the other, *De Schreeuw* (the Scream), honours free speech and, more specifically, filmmaker Theo van Gogh, who was murdered at the southeast corner of the park in 2004 (p169). Another (living) monument to Van Gogh is the Spreek-steen, an open-forum 'speakers' corner' established on the park's east side in 2005 – scheduled talks (almost always in Dutch) are held on Sundays at 1.30pm.

TROPENMUSEUM

☎ 568 82 15; www.tropenmuseum.nl; Linnaeusstraat 2; adult/child under 6yr/child 6-17yr/senior or student €7.50/free/4/6; 🕑 10am-5pm; 🚊 9/10/14 Alexanderplein; ♿

You could spend all day in this utterly absorbing anthropology museum, watching Bollywood clips, peering through windows into faux bazaar stalls and listening to hits on the Mexican jukebox. The museum began as a collection of colonial booty, so the areas covering former Dutch territory are particularly rich, with gorgeous Indonesian jewellery and enormous Polynesian war canoes. The onsite cafe features dishes from around the globe, but you can also head to a neighbourhood restaurant for the real deal.

SHOP

DAPPERMARKT
Street Market

Dapperstraat btwn Mauritskade & Wijttenbachstraat; 🕑 9am-5pm Mon-Sat; 🚊 3/7 Dapperstraat

Reflecting the Oost's diverse immigrant population, the Dappermarkt is a delight, a heart-warming mix of people, food and multipacks of socks. Though it was crowned the Netherlands' best street market in 2008, on the surface it doesn't seem much different from the Albert Cuypmarkt (p106). To really appreciate the place, don't bother with any actual shopping – just stroll and ogle the crowd.

EAT

ELKAAR *French*　　　€€€

☎ 330 75 59; Alexanderplein 6; 🕑 lunch Sun-Fri, dinner daily; 🚊 9/10/14 Alexanderplein

On a quiet corner by a canal, this small, elegant restaurant does

Head to De Ijsbreker for a touch of class and loads of *gezelligheid*

wonderful things with seafood, and applies truffle shavings liberally. There's a two-course lunch special too – a treat before or after the Tropenmuseum.

PATA NEGRA Spanish €€
☎ 692 25 06; Reinwardtstraat 1; noon-midnight Sun-Thu, noon-1am Fri & Sat; 3/7/9 Linnaeusstraat
A branch of the Utrechtsestraat tapas joint (p89).

ROOPRAM ROTI
Surinamese €
☎ 061 475 82 00; 1e Van Swindenstraat 4; lunch & dinner; 9 1e Van Swindenstraat; V

There's often a line to the door at this bare-bones and super-delicious takeout Surinamese place, but don't worry – it moves fast. Place your order – lamb roti 'extra' (with egg), and a *barra* (lentil doughnut), at least – with the man at the bar, and don't forget the hot sauce.

TRINBAGO Caribbean €€
☎ 061 469 39 87; 1e Van Swindenstraat 44; dinner Wed-Mon; 9 1e Van Swindenstraat; V
West Indian cuisine gets dressed up – and very nicely too. Spicy dishes such as callaloo (a tasty green-leaf vegetable) are cooked with a grandmother's soulful

touch, but plated with an artist's eye. 'Calvin's creations' – the chef-artist-owner's own work – dot the menu, and they're all good.

🍴 VILLA RUYSCH French €€
☎ 663 53 66; Ruyschstraat 15;
🕑 10am-10.30pm; 🚊 3 Wibautstraat;
♿ Ⓥ 🚻
The Oost is short on stylish eateries, so this grand cafe stands out. Particularly nice is its package breakfast: eggs baked with cheese, a perfectly flaky croissant and homemade preserves. At night, it's on to cocktails and a menu of French bistro fare. There's lots of outdoor seating, but then you'd

miss out on the gorgeous interior, which glitters with Murano-glass mosaics and other flash details.

🍴 VISHANDEL RINKOEN
Seafood €
☎ 463 11 18; Sumatrastraat 98;
🕑 9am-4.30pm Mon-Sat; 🚊 3/7
Muiderpoortstation
Like other Moroccan-run fish shops in this neighbourhood, this one doubles as a restaurant – pick out what you like from the case and it's cooked up and served at the tables in the next room. Whole prawns arrive in garlicky sauce, calamari is delectably fried and the fish soup is rich – and it all comes in at about €10 per person.

WORTH THE TRIP
Feeling vegetable-deprived after a steady diet of *frites*? The best antidote to a FEBO binge is the lovely restaurant **De Kas** (☎ 462 45 62; www.restaurantdekas.nl; Kamerlingh Onneslaan 3, Frankendael Park; 🕑 noon-2pm Mon-Fri, 6.30-10pm Mon-Sat; ♿ Ⓥ), set in a glittering 19th-century greenhouse. The restaurant grows its own produce, both in the greenhouse (ask for a tour) and in a farm plot near the city, and picks it fresh each morning to compose the single set menu – five courses at dinner (€47.50), four at lunch (€35). Meat and fish are responsibly sourced and exceptionally delicious, while vegetarians (mention your preference when you book) are treated very well.

🍸 DRINK
🍸 DE IJSBREKER Brown Cafe
☎ 468 18 08; Weesperzijde 23; 🕑 9am-1am Sun-Thu, 9am-2am Fri & Sat; 🚊 3
Wibautstraat; Ⓥ 🚻
Pull up a chair on the terrace at this lovely cafe on the Amstel and it's hard to decide whether to face the beautiful buildings or the gleaming river lined with houseboats. Inside used to house a major jazz and avant-garde music club – that institution has become the Muziekgebouw aan 't IJ (p139), leaving more room here for drinkers in the plush booths and along the marble bar.

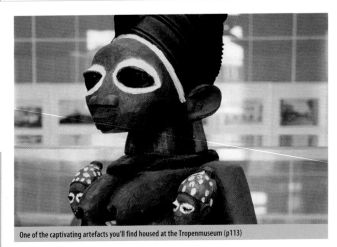

One of the captivating artefacts you'll find housed at the Tropenmuseum (p113)

⭐ PLAY

⭐ CANVAS OP DE 7E *Nightclub*

☎ 716 38 17; www.canvasopde7e.nl, in Dutch; Wibautstraat 150; 🕐 noon-1am, to 3am Fri & Sat; 🚇 3 Wibautstraat; ♿

Take the elevator to the 7th floor for this restaurant-bar-club. Edgy and improvisational, it's the social centre for all the artists with studios in this building, the former *Volkskrant* newspaper office. The sunset view is terrific, heightened by highly creative cocktails for just €5. Check the website for the event schedule and to make sure it's open – these city-approved *broedplaats* (breeding ground) projects often last only a few years.

⭐ STUDIO K *Arts Centre*

☎ 692 04 22; www.studio-k.nu; Timorplein 62; 🚇 14 Zeeburgerdijk; ♿ 🚻

Sporting two cinemas, space for bands and theatre, an eclectic Greek-Spanish restaurant (open for lunch and dinner from Tuesday to Sunday) and a huge terrace, the student-run Studio K is your one-stop shop for hip culture in the Oost. Stop in for a coffee, and you might wind up staying for a dance party…

⭐ TO NIGHT *Nightclub*

☎ 850 24 00; www.hotelarena.nl; 's-Gravesandestraat 51; 🕐 Thu-Sat; 🚇 3/7 Beukenweg

Hotel Arena's club hosts radically different nights from one evening to the next, from salsa to '90s hits. It's a bit out of the centre, but definitely worth a hike, as your €15-or-less ticket gets you entry into one of the most beautiful spaces in Amsterdam – a marble-trimmed chapel. As an added bonus, the drinks are relatively cheap.

⭐ **TROPENTHEATER** *Concert Hall*
☎ **568 85 00; www.tropentheater.nl; Linnaeusstraat 2;** 🚊 **9/10/14 Alexanderplein;** ♿ ⚹
Two halls adjoining the Tropenmuseum welcome performers from Cuba, Lebanon, Kurdistan and beyond. Check the website for schedule and ticket prices.

>NIEUWMARKT & PLANTAGE

The old centre ends and the more modern city begins at the Nieuwmarkt, a plaza dominated by the ominous-looking Waag, once a city gate, then a weigh house and now one of the many cafes (In de Waag, p129) that make this square a popular afternoon and evening hangout.

To the southeast, Jodenbreestraat leads into the old Jewish quarter. Little remains, in part due to a controversial overhaul in the 1980s, but a few museums and monuments commemorate the community that once flourished here and in the Plantage neighbourhood further east. Laid out as a garden district in the late 17th century, the Plantage was built up only around 1850, and it's still one of the greenest parts of the city. It's bordered to the north by Entrepotdok, a string of nearly 100 19th-century warehouses, also renovated in the 1980s – to much better effect.

A portion of this area is not served by trams; bus and metro details are provided, but the Nieuwmarkt is not a long walk from the Dam or Waterlooplein.

NIEUWMARKT & PLANTAGE

👁 SEE
Artis Zoo	**1**	E4
Chiellerie	**2**	A3
Hollandsche Schouwburg	**3**	D4
Hortus Botanicus	**4**	D4
Joods Historisch Museum	**5**	B4
Portuguese-Israelite Synagogue	**6**	C4
Rembrandthuis	**7**	B3
Scheepvaarthuis	**8**	C1
Verzetsmuseum	**9**	E4
Wertheim Park	**10**	D4
Zuiderkerk	**11**	A3

🏠 SHOP
De Beestenwinkel	**12**	A4
Droog	**13**	A4

Het Fort van Sjakoo	**14**	B4
Joe's Vliegerwinkel	**15**	A3
't Klompenhuisje	**16**	A3
Waterlooplein Flea Market	**17**	B4

🍴 EAT
Café Bern	**18**	B2
Café Kadijk	**19**	E3
De Tokoman	**20**	B4
Éénvistweevis	**21**	E3
Frenzi	**22**	A4
Greetje	**23**	C2
Hemelse Modder	**24**	B2
In de Waag	**25**	B2
Koffiehuis van den Volksbond	**26**	D3
Nam Kee	**27**	B2

Plancius	**28**	E4
Toko Joyce	**29**	A2

🍷 DRINK
Brouwerij 't IJ	**30**	H4
De Doelen	**31**	A4
De Engelbewaarder	**32**	A3
De Sluyswacht	**33**	B3
Greenhouse	**34**	B4
Lokaal 't Loosje	**35**	A2

⭐ PLAY
Amsterdams Marionetten Theater	**36**	B2
Het Muziektheater	**37**	B4
TunFun	**38**	C4

Please see over for map

SEE

ARTIS ZOO

☎ 523 34 00; www.artis.nl; Plantage Kerklaan 38-40; adult/senior/child 3-9yr/child under 3yr €17.50/16.50/14/free; ⏰ 9am-5pm Sep-May, 9am-6pm Sun-Fri, 9am-sunset Sat Jun-Aug; 🚊 9/14 Plantage Kerklaan; ♿ 👶

Founded in 1838, this zoo feels a bit cramped for modern tastes, but the old buildings (some from the earliest days of the Plantage) are beautiful and the grounds are lush. Plus it's heaven for kids, with more than 700 animal species. One genius exhibit: the murky canal cross-section in the aquarium, featuring discarded bikes and creepy eels. If you prefer your nature pinned to a board or stuffed, be sure to stop by the zoo's museum, a trove of taxidermy and other 19th-century relics. You can actually see into part of the zoo from Entrepotdok, just to the north – see if you can spot the oryx and the zebras!

CHIELLERIE

☎ 320 94 48; www.chiellerie.nl; Raamgracht 58; ⏰ 2-6pm; 🚊 9/14 Waterlooplein

A very democratic gallery, Chiellerie is open to anyone who wants to mount an exposition – the result is occasionally awful, but never as amateur as you'd expect.

Amsterdam's younger artists make good use of the space.

HOLLANDSCHE SCHOUWBURG

☎ 531 03 40; www.hollandscheschouwburg.nl; Plantage Middenlaan 24; ⏰ 11am-4pm; admission free; 🚊 9/14 Plantage Kerklaan

Located in the Jewish quarter, the 1892 Dutch Theatre was renamed the Jewish Theatre by the Nazis in 1941, then used as a deportation centre. Thousands of Jews were sent to death camps from here, and a memorial and exhibition describes this period.

HORTUS BOTANICUS

☎ 625 90 21; www.dehortus.nl; Plantage Middenlaan 2a; admission €7/3.50; ⏰ 9am-5pm Feb-Jun & Sep-Nov, 9am-7pm Jul & Aug, 9am-4pm Dec & Jan; 🚊 9/14 Mr Visserplein; ♿

Built in 1682, the Hortus Botanicus began as a breeding ground for exotic species collected by the VOC (Dutch East India Company). Despite its history, the place is rather small and not as lush as you'd expect.

There is an interesting collection of South African plants, the world's oldest potted plant (more than 300 years, and looking it), a clever semicircular garden representing the plant kingdom and a pretty cafe. A garden shop sells

NEIGHBOURHOODS

NIEUWMARKT & PLANTAGE

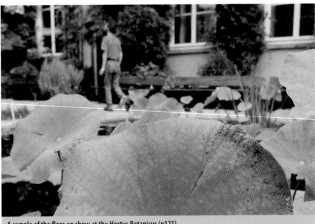
A sample of the flora on show at the Hortus Botanicus (p121)

items like clog-shaped terracotta pots.

JOODS HISTORISCH MUSEUM

Jewish Historical Museum; ☎ 531 03 10; www.jhm.nl; Nieuwe Amstelstraat 1; admission €7.50/3; ⏱ 11am-5pm; 🚊 9/14 Waterlooplein; ♿
The Great Synagogue, dating from 1675, holds exhibits on the Jewish Diaspora in the Netherlands, as well as the pillars of Judaism. Perhaps what's most revealing is the room filled with cultural ephemera, which illustrates the Jewish influence in Dutch society – from HEMA stores to the Ajax football team.

PORTUGUESE-ISRAELITE SYNAGOGUE

☎ 624 53 51; www.esnoga.com; Mr Visserplein 3; admission €6.50/4; ⏱ 10am-4pm Sun-Fri Apr-Oct, 10am-4pm Sun-Thu, 10am-2pm Fri Sep-Mar; 🚊 9/14 Mr Visserplein
'Hidden' behind a row of single-storey buildings, as per Calvinist policy, this was the largest synagogue in Europe when it was completed in 1675. Its enormous piers were inspired by a model of the Temple of Solomon in Jerusalem (on display at the Bijbels Museum, p62). The interior is austere, with sand on the floorboards and flickering brass chandeliers. If you're visiting the Joods Historisch

Museum (opposite) as well, get the combo ticket for €10/5.

REMBRANDTHUIS
☎ 520 04 00; www.rembrandthuis.nl; Jodenbreestraat 4; adult/under 6yr/6-15yr/student €8/free/1.50/5.50; ⏱ 10am-5pm; 🚊 9/14 Waterlooplein; ♿

Rembrandt van Rijn (1606–69) lived and worked in this building for almost 20 years, until poverty forced him into a dumpy flat in the Jordaan. His light-filled studio is the highlight, laid out as though he's just nipped down to the kitchen for a bite to eat. Another room is crammed with the art and curiosities that Rembrandt collected – seashells, dried insects, animal horns, busts of Roman emperors and work by other artists. A rotating selection of Rembrandt's etchings is also on display.

SCHEEPVAARTHUIS
Shipping House; Prins Hendrikkade 108; 🚌 22/32/33/34 Prins Hendrikkade; ♿

This dark-brick building, built in 1916, was the first true example of Amsterdam School style – and it's still one of the grandest, encrusted in elaborate nautical detailing. Step inside (it's a luxury hotel now) to admire stained glass, gorgeous light fixtures and an amazing staircase.

VERZETSMUSEUM
☎ 620 25 35; www.verzetsmuseum.org; Plantage Kerklaan 61; adult/child under 6yr/7-15yr €6.50/free/3.50; ⏱ 10am-5pm Tue-Fri, 11am-5pm Sat-Mon; 🚊 9/14 Plantage Kerklaan; ♿

This museum honours the work of the Dutch Resistance and documents gestures large (such as the 1941 dockworkers' strike) and small (document forgery). But it doesn't shy away from the truth that the majority of Dutch Jews were killed during WWII; one chilling display articulates the various reasons many people refused to shelter Jews. Just as interesting is the smaller wing devoted to the Resistance in the Dutch East Indies, which soon after led to independence for Indonesia.

WERTHEIM PARK
Plantage Parklaan; ⏱ dawn-dusk; 🚊 9/14 Mr Visserplein

Opposite the Hortus Botanicus, this is a willow-shaded spot by a canal. Its most significant feature is the Auschwitz Memorial, designed by Dutch writer Jan Wolkers: a panel of broken mirrors installed in the ground reflects the sky.

ZUIDERKERK
☎ 622 29 62; Zuiderkerkhof 72; ⏱ 9am-4pm Mon-Fri, noon-4pm Sat; Ⓜ Nieuwmarkt; ♿

Amsterdam's first Protestant church (1611) was used as a

morgue during the 'Hunger Winter' of WWII. Now it's a city-run info centre for Amsterdam's various urban expansion schemes – basically an explanation for all the construction around town. (Fittingly, next door is the Pentagon, a dreadful 1980s housing complex and mute warning against future bad planning.)

🏠 SHOP

🏠 DE BEESTENWINKEL
Children's

☎ 623 18 05; www.beestenwinkel .nl, in Dutch; Staalstraat 11; 🚊 9/14 **Waterlooplein**

From teeny-tiny teddies to pink plastic pig snouts, this shop is packed to the rafters with *de best* (best) of *de beesten* (animals).

🏠 DROOG
Design

☎ 523 50 59; Staalstraat 7b; 🕐 noon-6pm Tue-Sun; 🚊 4/9/14/16/24/25 **Muntplein**

Droog means 'dry' in Dutch, and this design house's products are strong on dry wit. The shop is one part playground – there's a big garden swing, and a surprising bench – and one part gallery, which displays limited-edition pieces. But even small items, like superpowerful suction hooks, are seriously smart.

🏠 HET FORT VAN SJAKOO
Books

☎ 625 89 79; Jodenbreestraat 24; 🕐 11am-6pm Mon-Fri, 11am-5pm Sat; 🚊 9/14 **Waterlooplein**

Get the low-down on the squat scene, plus locally produced zines and Trotsky translations, at this lefty bookshop, which has been in operation since 1977.

🏠 JOE'S VLIEGERWINKEL
Children's

☎ 625 01 39; Nieuwe Hoogstraat 19; Ⓜ **Nieuwmarkt**

If it flies, it's in stock at this kite specialist – pick up a colourful starter model for the kids or a

Sort trash from treasure at Waterloopleinmarkt

NIEUWMARKT & PLANTAGE

FREE MARKET(S)

In addition to the farmers' market and clothes vending on Noordermarkt (p67), Amsterdam has several other interesting street markets that occur periodically. Look out for:
> **Antiques** Nieuwmarkt (Map pp122–3, B2; 9am-5pm Sun May-Sep); Amstelveld (Map pp82–3, F4; 9am-6pm last Fri of the month May-Aug)
> **Organic produce** Nieuwmarkt (Map pp122–3, B2; 9am-3pm Sat), Haarlemmer-plein (Map pp60–1, C1; 9am-2pm Wed)
> **Books** Spui (Map pp38–9, B7; 8am-6pm Fri)
> **Plants** Amstelveld (Map pp82–3, F4; 8.30am-1pm Mon Mar-Dec)

deluxe Chinese dragon fighter, and head out to the Museumplein (p96).

'T KLOMPENHUISJE
Footwear, Children's
622 81 00; Nieuwe Hoogstraat 9a; Mon-Sat; M Nieuwmarkt
Finely crafted and surprisingly comfortable, traditional Dutch *klompen* (clogs) are just the thing to potter around the garden in. The shop also stocks lots of children's shoes.

WATERLOOPLEINMARKT
Antiques, Clothing
Waterlooplein; 9am-5pm Mon-Sat; 9/14 Waterlooplein;
This flea market next to the Stopera (p131) is the place to pick up a funky vintage ensemble, trawl through piles of €1 clothing, haggle over dented antiques or stock your hippy van with tie-dye bedspreads and a brand-new bong. Don't go too late – by 4.30pm,

vendors are more interested in packing up than making a sale.

EAT

CAFÉ BERN *Swiss* €€
622 00 34; Nieuwmarkt 9; dinner; M Nieuwmarkt; V
People have been flocking to this well-worn brown cafe for more than 40 years to indulge in gruyère fondue and entrecôte. It's generally closed for a large part of the summer, but do you really want fondue in hot weather anyway?

CAFÉ KADIJK *Indonesian* €
0617-744 44 11; Kadijksplein 5; noon-10pm; 22/42/43/359 Plantage Kerklaan
This hip split-level cafe looks like it can serve no more than coffee from its tiny kitchen, but in fact it does quite good Indonesian food. Go for the *Eitjes van Tante Bea*, a spicy mix of egg, shrimp and beans, as well as the rich *rendang*

curry. And because it's a cafe, there's *appeltaart* for dessert.

DE TOKOMAN *Surinamese* €
☎ 421 56 36; Waterlooplein 327; ◷ 11am-7.30pm Mon-Sat; 🚊 9/14 Waterlooplein; Ⓥ ⚥
We have it on good authority that this is the city's best *broodje pom*, a sandwich filled with a tasty mash of chicken and a starchy Surinamese tuber. You'll want the *zuur* (pickled-cabbage relish) and *peper* (chilli) on it, plus a cold can of coconut water to wash it down. Still hungry? Descend into the Waterlooplein metro stop to rival De Hapjeshoek and nab a *chili kip* or *zoutvlees* sandwich.

ÉÉNVISTWEEVIS *Seafood* €€
☎ 623 28 94; Schippersgracht 6; ◷ 6-10pm Tue-Sun; 🚌 22/42/43/359 Kadijksplein; ⚥
This unassuming local favourite has a short, handwritten menu of whatever's fresh from the sea. The service is slow and the restaurant gets noisy, but it's all about the great oysters, soup and simply prepared mains, such as sole in butter.

FRENZI *Mediterranean* €€
☎ 423 51 12; Zwanenburgwal 232; ◷ 8.30am-11pm Mon-Fri, 10am-11pm Sat & Sun; 🚊 9/14 Waterlooplein; ⚥ Ⓥ ⚥

After a Waterlooplein market (p127) expedition, refuel at this nearby cafe-restaurant with a big, creative sandwich (the *vitello tonnato* – veal in tuna sauce – on bread is genius!) or plate of pasta, and perhaps a sweet from noted patisserie Holtkamp (handier than visiting the shop's Vijzelgracht location).

GREETJE
Dutch €€€
☎ 779 74 50; www.restaurantgreetje .nl; Peperstraat 23-25; ◷ dinner Tue-Sun; Ⓜ Nieuwmarkt; Ⓥ
Elegant Greetje will make you reconsider Dutch cuisine. Never mind *stamppot* – here you'll see traditional dishes like leek soup, pickled mackerel and braised oxtail, all composed of market-fresh ingredients and presented beautifully.

HEMELSE MODDER
Dutch €€
☎ 624 32 03; Oude Waal 11; ◷ dinner Tue-Sun; Ⓜ Nieuwmarkt; ⚥ Ⓥ
Celery-green walls and blond-wood tables are the backdrop for equally light and unpretentious food, which emphasises North Sea fish and farm-fresh produce. If there's no berry pudding for dessert, the namesake *hemelse modder* (heavenly mud) chocolate mousse is a good fallback.

🍴 IN DE WAAG
International €€

☎ 422 77 72; Nieuwmarkt 4; ⏱ 10am-midnight; Ⓜ Nieuwmarkt; ♿ Ⓥ 👶
Prime seats in the centre of the Nieuwmarkt give you a great view of the scene, but don't miss the candlelit interior of this massive historic building. The lunch sandwiches are enormous and there's a good selection of hot dishes beyond that; for dinner though, the prices are unjustifiably high.

🍴 KOFFIEHUIS VAN DEN VOLKSBOND
International €€

☎ 622 12 09; Kadijksplein 4; ⏱ dinner; 🚊 22/42/43/359 Plantage Kerklaan; Ⓥ 👶
What began life as a charitable coffee house for dockworkers later got revived by squatters. It still has a fashionably grungy vibe – wood floors, a giant red-rose mural and tall candles on the tables. The ever-changing menu has huge plates of comfort food with ingredients like mussels and Moroccan sausage.

🍴 NAM KEE *Chinese* €

☎ 638 28 48; Gelderskade 447; ⏱ noon-11pm; Ⓜ Nieuwmarkt; Ⓥ
Arguably the nicer branch of Amsterdam's Chinese icon (see p51).

🍴 PLANCIUS
Mediterranean €€

☎ 330 94 69; Plantage Kerklaan 61; ⏱ 11am-11pm; 🚊 9/14 Plantage Kerklaan; Ⓥ 👶
This industrial-chic converted garage offers some nice alternatives to standard sandwiches at lunch: a big messy lamb burger, a great mixed salad, a pasta dish or two. Dinner dishes tend towards upmarket comfort food. The clientele is mostly TV execs who work nearby.

🍴 TOKO JOYCE *Indonesian* €

☎ 427 90 91; Nieuwmarkt 38; ⏱ 11am-8pm Tue-Sat, 4-8pm Sun & Mon; Ⓜ Nieuwmarkt; Ⓥ 👶
At this takeaway place, pick and mix a platter of Surinamese-Indonesian food from the glass case – start with spiced yellow rice and add various spicy, coconutty stews. Get a wedge of *spekkoek*, a moist layered gingerbread, to finish.

🍸 DRINK
🍸 BROUWERIJ 'T IJ *Beer Bar*

☎ 622 83 25; Funenkade 7; ⏱ 3-8pm Wed-Sun; 🚊 10 Hoogte Kadijk
A *de rigueur* photo op, plus beer! The tasting room of Amsterdam's leading microbrewery has a cosy, down-and-dirty beer-hall feel, and the house brew is delicious. It just

NIEUWMARKT & PLANTAGE

NO, YOU'RE NOT DRUNK…

Those buildings *are* leaning. Some (like the Sluyswacht, below) have simply shifted over the centuries, but many canal houses were deliberately constructed to tip forward. Interior staircases were narrow, so owners needed an easy way to move large goods and furniture to the upper floors. The solution: a hoist built into the gable, to lift objects up and in through the windows. The tilt allows loading without bumping into the house front. The forward lean also makes the houses seem larger, which makes it easier to admire the facade and gable – a fortunate coincidence for everyone.

so happens to be at the foot of De Gooyer Windmill, an 18th-century grain mill and the last of five that stood in this area.

DE DOELEN *Brown Cafe*
☎ 624 90 23; Kloveniersburgwal 125; ⏲ 8am-1am Mon-Thu, 8am-2am Fri & Sat; 🚊 4/9/14/16/24/25 Muntplein
On a busy crossroads between the Amstel and De Wallen (the red-light district), this cafe dates back to 1895 and looks it: carved wooden goat's head, stained-glass lamps, sand on the floor. But there's a fun, youthful atmosphere, and during fine weather the tables spill across the street for picture-perfect canal views.

DE ENGELBEWAARDER
Brown Cafe
☎ 625 37 72; Kloveniersburgwal 59; 🚊 9/14 Waterlooplein
If you like jazz, plan on spending a Sunday afternoon (from 4.30pm) at this small cafe, which has been hosting an open session for

decades. The rest of the week, it's a mellow, old-fashioned place to enjoy a beer by the sunny windows.

DE SLUYSWACHT
Brown Cafe
☎ 625 76 11; Jodenbreestraat 1; 🚊 9/14 Waterlooplein
Listing like a ship in a high wind, this tiny black building was once a lock-keeper's house. Today the canalside terrace is one of the nicest spots in town to down a beer, especially after trawling the Waterlooplein market (p127).

GREENHOUSE *Coffeeshop*
☎ 622 54 99; Waterlooplein 345; ⏲ 9am-1am Sun-Thu, 9am-2am Fri & Sat; 🚊 9/14 Waterlooplein
A branch of the excellent operation in De Pijp (p111), this place has a 21-plus door policy.

LOKAAL 'T LOOSJE
Brown Cafe
☎ 627 26 35; Nieuwmarkt 32-34; Ⓜ Nieuwmarkt

With its beautiful etched-glass windows and tile tableaux on the walls, this is one of the oldest and prettiest cafes in the Nieuwmarkt area – as good a place as any to settle in and watch the action on the square.

⭐ PLAY

⭐ AMSTERDAMS MARIONETTEN THEATER *Theatre*

☎ 620 80 27; www.marionettentheater.nl; Nieuwe Jonkerstraat 8; adult/child 8-14 €12.50/7.50; Ⓜ Nieuwmarkt; &

This puppet theatre performs Mozart operas such as *The Magic Flute*, enthralling kids (eight years old and up) and adults alike with the fairy-tale stage sets, period costumes and beautiful singing. Shows are roughly twice a month.

⭐ HET MUZIEKTHEATER *Concert Hall*

☎ 625 54 55; www.hetmuziektheater.nl; Waterlooplein 22; ⊙ box office 10am-6pm Mon-Sat; 🚊 9/14 Waterlooplein; &

The opera house adjoining Amsterdam's city hall (hence its nickname, Stopera: *stadhuis* plus *opera*) is home to the Netherlands National Ballet and the Netherlands Opera. On the east side of the building, a small exhibit surrounds the Normal Amsterdams Peil, the not-exactly-sea-level point on which all construction in the country is calculated. A somewhat alarming diorama shows just how much of the city is below the line.

⭐ TUNFUN *Playground*

☎ 689 43 00; www.tunfun.nl; Mr Visserplein 7; admission free/€7.50; ⊙ 10am-6pm; 🚊 9/14 Mr Visserplein; &

An ingenious reuse of a traffic underpass, TunFun is a massive indoor playground, perfect for rainy Amsterdam days. Kids aged one to 12 can build, climb, roll, draw, play indoor soccer and dance, while parents relax in the cafe. Kids must be accompanied by an adult.

If you're so inclined, drop into De Sluyswacht

>HARBOUR & EASTERN DOCKLANDS

In just a decade, Amsterdam has completely remade its harbour. What used to be the city's fringe – both physically and culturally – has become a centre for culture and sleek modern living. All straight lines and open vistas, the neighbourhood is invigorating to visit if only as a contrast to the city centre, but you'll also want to come out here for a concert at the Muziekgebouw aan 't IJ (p139).

The mighty green NEMO (opposite), erected in 1997, started the new era. Old warehouses and loading docks were gutted and new projects commissioned. Some of the housing blocks can be grim on a grey day, but don't miss the jaunty mismatched blocks on the west end of Java-eiland, the angular silver building dubbed 'the Whale' (at the west end of Sporenburg) and the swooping red footbridge between Borneo-eiland and Sporenburg.

This area is less compact, so it's rewarding and easy to cover by bicycle. There are relatively few bars and cafes, but those that are here make the most of their dramatic location.

HARBOUR & EASTERN DOCKLANDS

Please see over for map

◑ SEE

◑ ARCAM

☎ 620 48 78; www.arcam.nl; Prins Hendrikkade 600; ☽ 1-5pm Tue-Sat; 🚌 32/33/34/35/359/361/363 IJ-Tunnel

Located in a stunningly shaped building, Amsterdam's Centre for Architecture (ARCAM) should be the first point of call for architecture and urban design buffs. Staff can suggest buildings to see to match your interests, while the centre also holds regular exhibitions on Dutch and international architecture.

◑ NEDERLANDS SCHEEPVAARTMUSEUM

Netherlands Maritime Museum; ☎ 523 22 22; www.scheepvaartmuseum.nl; Kattenburgerplein 1; 🚌 22/43 Kattenburgerplein

At the time of research the Scheepvaartmuseum was closed for renovation and not scheduled to reopen until the end of 2010. Its full-scale replica of the 700-tonne *Amsterdam* ship is moored by the NEMO (below).

◑ NEMO

☎ 531 32 33; www.e-nemo.nl; Oosterdok 2; adult/under 4yr €11.50/free; ☽ 10am-5pm Tue-Sun Sep-Jun, daily Jul-Aug; 🚌 32/33/34/35/359/361/363 IJ-Tunnel; ♿

Jutting into the harbour like a ship, Renzo Piano's stunning green-copper edifice is an excellent science and technology museum with hands-on laboratories. On the walk down to the museum, look out for a whole collection of restored cargo ships; you can also visit a beautiful replica of the *Amsterdam* ship (€5, or €15 including NEMO entrance), staffed with grubby-looking pirates who sing sea shanties and conduct burials at sea every hour. NEMO's stepped roof (admission free) is the city's largest summer terrace.

With a building like this, it's not hard to find NEMO

NOORD

A B C D

32, 38, 39

1

IJ Tunnel

Tunnel

2

IJpleinveer

32, 39

Java-
eiland   42

3

Piet Heinkade

17 ⟨⟩ 22   Passenger
⟨⟩ 20   Terminal
Amsterdam

Vriesseveem

Jollemanhof 11

Javabrug

25, 26   23   326

Oosterdoksstr

Piet Heinkade

Dijksgracht

21
4

Oosterdokskade

4

P
Prins Hendrikkade

Oosterdok

Oosterdok

2

3

EASTERN
ISLANDS

Kattenburg

Kattenburgerstr

Kattenburgergracht

Wittenburg

Grote Wittenburgerstr

Kleine Wittenburgerstr

Oostenburg

22, 42, 43

NIEUWMARKT

Oude Schans

Tunnel

Rapenburg

Mediamatic
Supermarket

Nieuwe Uilenburgergracht

Uilenburgerstr

Kadijkpl

Nieuwe Vaart

Wittenburgergracht

2

1

Wittenburgerstr

Overhalsgang

Waalgat

Wittenburgervaart

Oostenburgergr

Oostenburgervoorstr

Nieuwe Vaart

12

See Nieuwmarkt
& Plantage
Map pp122-3

5

Valkenburgerstr

Rapenburgerstr

9, 14
Muiderstr

Plantage Kade

Plantage
Parklaan

Hoogte Kadijk

Laagte Kadijk

Binnenkadijk

Entrepotdok

6

M
Weesperstr

Wertheimpark

Plantage
Middenlaan

P
Artis
Planetarium

Sarphatistr 10

IJtunnelkade

22

Hortusplantsoen

Plantage Kerklaan

9, 14

PLANTAGE

Artis
Library

Artis Zoo

Artis Zoological
Museum

E F G H

1

SCHELLINGWOUDE

0   400 m
0   0.2 miles

2

Het IJ

3

...rakade
Sumatrakade
Surinamekade
8 ▢ 7 ▢ 14 ▢
KNSM-laan
▮ 10
KNSM-
eiland
▢ 5 ▮ 18 ▢ 9
Levantkade

Veemkade
Oostelijke Handelskade
IJ Haven
▮ 23
Lloydplein
▮ 16 ▮ 19
Rietlanden
Sporenburg
Keesje
Brijdeplantsoen
10
Verbindingsdam
▮ 6
15
26, 326
4

Tunnel   26
59
43
ZEEBURG
Borneo-
eiland
Borneolaan
Borneokade
Czaar Peterstr
C. van Eesterenlaan

5

▮ 13
Cruquiusweg
43, 59
Zeeburgerkade
Zeeburgerpad

Singelgracht
Zeeburgerdijk
See Oosterpark
& Around
Map pp114-5
22
14   DAPPERBUURT

6

OPENBARE BIBLIOTHEEK AMSTERDAM

Amsterdam Public Library; ☎ 523 09 00; www.oba.nl; Oosterdokskade 143; ⏲ 10am-10pm; 🚊 25/26 Muziekgebouw; ♿
This nine-storey 'tower of knowledge' redefines the public library as a social point as much as a place for reading. Big, inviting couches are scattered around every floor of the light-filled building, there are scads of free internet terminals, and the cafe on the top floor (an outlet of La Place, p50) also offers a beautiful view.

🛍 SHOP

DE ODE *Speciality Shop*
☎ 419 08 82; Levantkade 51; ⏲ by appointment only; 🚊 10 Azartplein
Send your loved ones off in style, with a creative casket from this one-of-a-kind shop. Open by appointment only, but a couple of interesting options are always on display in the window.

JC CREATIONS *Clothing*
☎ 419 72 20; Baron GA Tindalstraat 150; ⏲ 11am-6pm Tue-Fri, 11am-5pm Sat; 🚊 10 C van Eesterenlaan
Take a deep breath when you enter this small shop: classy corsets are the speciality. Plenty of ready-made options, and custom orders welcome.

KEET IN HUIS *Children's*
☎ 419 59 58; KNSM-laan 297; ⏲ Tue-Sun; 🚊 10 Azartplein
At this two-storey emporium, the young ones frolic in the play area while their superhip parents pick up Bugaboo strollers, funky room decor, nappy bags with flair and oodles of adorable clothing.

POL'S POTTEN *Design*
☎ 419 35 41; KNSM-laan 39; ⏲ Tue-Sun; 🚊 10 Azartplein
How do new residents in this style-conscious district furnish their new apartments? They head straight to this large interior-design shop, which has some particularly nice ceramic work.

SISSY-BOY
Clothing, Housewares
☎ 419 15 59; KNSM-laan 19; ⏲ 8am-7pm Mon-Sat, 11am-7pm Sun; 🚊 10 Azartplein
A vast branch of the higher-end clothing-and-house-goodies chain (p47).

🍴 EAT

DE WERELDBOL
International   €
☎ 362 87 25; Piraeusplein 59; ⏲ 11am-9pm Tue-Fri, noon-9pm Sat & Sun; 🚊 10 Azartplein; V ♿
A passionate and personable owner-chef, an ever-changing

menu and a beautiful view of the water make this a nice place to end a day of sightseeing in this district. Note the early closing time.

🍴 EINDE VAN DE WERELD
Vegetarian   €

☎ 419 02 22; opposite Javakade 4; 🕑 from 7pm Wed & Fri; 🚊 10 Azartplein; V 👶

At the end of the world to Amsterdammers, look for the big yellow boat *Quo Vadis*. The volunteer-run onboard restaurant is cheap and very cheerful. Show up early, because you can't reserve, and when the food's gone, it's gone.

🍴 FIFTEEN *Italian*   €€€

☎ 0900 343 83 36; Jollemanhof 9; 🕑 dinner; 🚊 25 PTA; ♿

Following 'naked chef' Jamie Oliver's model for training underprivileged youth to cook, this industrial space is fun and scrawled with graffiti. Diners all get the same four-course menu, which changes weekly. Opinions are divided on the food and the enterprise, but our meal here was tasty and well executed.

🍴 FRANK'S SMOKEHOUSE
Sandwich Shop   €

☎ 670 07 74; Wittenburgergracht 303; 🕑 9am-4pm Mon, 9am-6pm Tue-Fri, 9am-5pm Sat; 🚊 10 1e Coehoornstraat, 🚌 22/43 Wittenburgergracht

Frank has a knack for smoked eel – and salmon, halibut, tuna and more. His little shop is primarily takeaway (you can get anything vacuum-packed, to carry through customs), but you can also sit down at the single table and have an excellent mackerel sandwich, bowl of soup or plate of charcuterie.

🍴 GARE DE L'EST
International   €€

☎ 463 06 20; Cruquiusweg 9; 🕑 dinner; 🚊 4 Zeeburgerdijk, 🚌 Stadsdeel Zeeburg

Gare de l'Est's four chefs are as eclectic as its rich Morocco-meets-Paris interior. We sampled a Mediterranean-influenced menu (other possibilities include North African or Asian), a single four-course menu of brilliantly prepared seafood and a beautiful cheese plate. Well worth the trek.

🍴 KOMPASZAAL *Cafe*   €

☎ 419 95 96; KNSM-laan 311; 🕑 11am-1am Wed-Sun; 🚊 10 Azartplein

Set in the century-old Royal Dutch Steamboat Company (KNSM in Dutch) arrivals hall, this cafe has a menu featuring Malaysian, Indian and Indonesian flavours. But the groovy green tiles and the water view from the balcony – a great spot for a beer – are even more captivating. On the ground floor, check out the scale models of the Eastern Docklands.

🍴 ROOS EN NOOR
International €

☎ 419 14 40; Baron GA Tindalstraat 148; ⏰ 4-9pm Mon-Fri, 3-8pm Sun; 🚊 10 C van Eesterenlaan

This chic little takeaway shop has a vast buffet, with prepared items like Chinese-spice duck and roasted beets, as well as full meals and sweets. It's a nice place to grab a late lunch or a sunset picnic while exploring the docklands' architecture.

🍴 SNEL *International* €€

☎ 561 36 77; Oostelijke Handelskade 34; ⏰ 7am-1am; 🚊 10 C van Eesterenlaan

We mention this restaurant not really for a full meal, but as an excuse to duck into the supremely cool Lloyd Hotel, set in the shell of a 1920s brick confection. The spacious restaurant serves snacks anytime of day, and has a great back garden.

🍴 STAR FERRY *Cafe* €€

☎ 788 20 90; www.starferry.nl, in Dutch; Piet Heinkade 1; ⏰ 10am-1am Sun-Thu, 10am-2am Fri & Sat; 🚊 25/26 Muziekgebouw; ♿ 🅥 👶

The flash cafe at the Muziekgebouw aan 't IJ is hard to beat for location and views. Several

SEE THE CITY ON THE CHEAP

For a bit of passive sightseeing, look no further than the tram; the lines rattle through great cross-sections of the city. One of the best routes is No 10, from near Westerpark, around the perimeter of the canal loop and out to the Eastern Docklands, passing 19th-century housing blocks, the Rijksmuseum (p98) and De Gooyer windmill (p129) along the way. Another good route is No 5, starting at Centraal Station and cutting south through the centre. The GVB offers a free English podcast tour for this route; download it from the 'Tourist Guide' section of www.gvb.nl.

storeys of glass take in the striking harbour panorama.

🍸 DRINK

🍸 KANIS & MEILAND *Cafe*

☎ 418 24 39; Levantkade 127; 🚊 10 Azartplein; 👶

As the first cafe in the neighbourhood, this roomy space has collected plenty of regulars, who sip coffee and spread out at the reading table. Outside seats take in a great view of the 'mainland'.

🍸 KHL *Cafe*

☎ 779 15 75; Oostelijke Handelskade 44; 🚊 10 C van Eesterenlaan; 👶

Just down from the Lloyd Hotel, KHL is a one-time squatter cafe gone legit. It's in a historic brick building – one of the few left in the area – and the garden is worth a glass or two. There's often eclectic music in the back room on weekends.

⭐ PLAY

⭐ BIMHUIS *Concert Hall*
☎ 788 21 88; www.bimhuis.nl; Piet Heinkade 3; tickets €12-20; 🚊 25/26 Muziekgebouw; ♿

The core of Amsterdam's influential jazz and improvisational music scene since 1973, the Bimhuis has kept its focus even after merging (architecturally) with the Muziekgebouw (right). Tuesdays at 10.30pm from September to June are an open jam session – fun and free.

⭐ CONSERVATORIUM VAN AMSTERDAM
Concert Hall
☎ 527 75 50; www.conservatorium vanamsterdam.nl; Oosterdokskade 151; 🚊 25/26 Muziekgebouw

The city's prestigious music school, set in a dramatic building on the harbour, is a great place to see affordable jazz, opera and classical performances, at very affordable prices.

⭐ MUZIEKGEBOUW AAN 'T IJ
Concert Hall
☎ 788 20 00; www.muziekgebouw .nl; Piet Heinkade 1; tickets €8.50-27.50; 🚊 25/26 Muziekgebouw; ♿

This magnificent building plays host to everything from the Holland Symfonia (which typically

The intriguing exterior of Amsterdam's Centre for Architecture (ARCAM; p133)

NEIGHBOURHOODS

HARBOUR & EASTERN DOCKLANDS

backs the national ballet) to the prestigious Metropole Orkest, which does smart arrangements of jazz and pop.

⭐ PANAMA
Nightclub, Live Music
☎ 311 86 86; www.panama.nl; Oostelijke Handelskade 4; 🚋 10/26 Rietlandpark

A full schedule of themed nights and international DJs sees Panama's club packed most nights, and it also books live music and comedy. Despite the Central American name the decor is Asian. The cocktails are fantastic.

>OUTER DISTRICTS

You wouldn't know it from the postcards, but Amsterdam extends well beyond the main canal rings. The city incorporates both dense urban housing projects and fields filled with cows – and it's all a surprisingly short bike, ferry or metro ride away. The areas described in the following pages can be visited in a few hours, or a trip can take the better part of a day, depending on your interests. The city's biggest green space, Amsterdam's 'worst' neighbourhood (which also has some of its best new architecture) and the part of the city that looks remarkably like the country – none of these spots have any notable museums or other typical sights, but they're the perfect change of pace from the close confines of the historic centre. And you're sure to return with a whole new perception of Amsterdam.

Boats moored on the Amstel River

OUTER DISTRICTS

DE BIJLMER

Blij in de Bijlmer! (Happy in the Bijlmer!) read the T-shirts worn by boosters of what was just a decade ago Amsterdam's most notorious neighbourhood, known for muggings, junkies and public housing gone wrong. No part of Amsterdam has changed so dramatically in such a short time. The city's largest Surinamese population lives here, along with immigrants from west and north Africa. A beautiful lake, Gaasper-plas, lies just to the south. And what used to be bleak Le Corbusier–inspired concrete is now a playground for some of the Netherlands' most innovative architects.

It's nice, but not necessary, to visit by bike, though the 30-minute ride from the city centre isn't particularly scenic. Hop on the metro (you can bring your wheels) to the dramatic Nicholas Grimshaw–designed

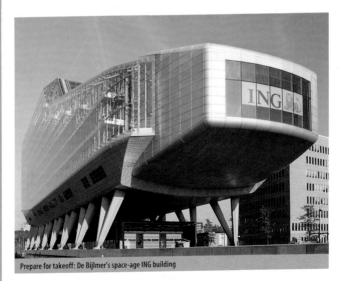

Prepare for takeoff: De Bijlmer's space-age ING building

Bijlmer station, opened in 2007. To the west lies **Ajax Stadium**, home of Amsterdam's revered football club. In the shopping plaza east of the tracks, just past the weird polygonal **ING building** (energy-efficient and 'green' in the '80s, well ahead of its time), look for the **Imagine IC** cultural centre, which dispenses excellent free audio tours of the area, as well as maps. From here, you can wind your way east, passing all kinds of novel structures, including a miniature version of the NEMO building (p133).

Eventually these give way to the few remaining **'honeycomb blocks'** of the original Bijlmer layout, each containing some 400 apartments. The 1960s brochures touted 'a modern city where the people of today can find the residential environment of tomorrow'. But the isolated, austere project rapidly lost lustre and, in the 1970s, the city began to funnel poor immigrants into the empty apartments. By the '80s, crime was common, and the infrastructure crumbling. Former residents lament the trash-filled lawns and broken elevators of those days, but many also wax nostalgic about the tight-knit community and the surrounding greenery.

In 1992 an El Al cargo plane crashed into two of the blocks, killing 43 people, many of them undocumented foreigners – a **memorial** stands in front of the missing buildings. The tragedy kick-started a re-evaluation of the neighbourhood that has shifted into wholesale rebuilding, and shifted the balance far in favour of privately owned property, rather than publicly managed apartments. Around the Kraaiennest metro stop, things still look pretty unreconstructed, except for the shiny **Taibah Mosque**, the first mosque built in the Netherlands, in 1984. The Ganzenhoef stop, due north, is a mix of old and new buildings, and home to a vibrant street market (on Saturdays) as well as a children's petting zoo, and a great Surinamese-Javanese restaurant, **De Smeltkroes**.

INFORMATION

Location 7.5km southeast of central Amsterdam
Getting there Ⓜ Bijlmer Arena, Ganzenhoef or Kraaiennest
Contact Imagine IC (☎ 489 48 66; www.imagineic.nl; Bijlmerplein 1006; ⏲ 11am-5pm Tue-Sat, 11am-9pm Thu)
Eating Kam Yin (☎ 409 58 88; Bijlmerplein 525; ⏲ 11am-9pm Mon-Sat, 3-9pm Sun), a branch of the Warmoesstraat restaurant (p50); De Smeltkroes (☎ 495 20 76; Bijlmerdreef 1289; ⏲ 10.30am-9.30pm Mon-Fri, 1-9.30pm Sat)

OUTER DISTRICTS

AMSTERDAM-NOORD

Even to most residents of Amsterdam, the north of the city is like another planet. But it's only a short ferry ride across the IJ to pretty old homes, isolated villages, open farmland and cows galore – all within the city limits. Everything's close enough for a day or afternoon bike ride; pick up a free Amsterdam-Noord map at one of the VVV (tourist board) offices at Centraal Station (p179).

Fans of derelict industry can head first for **NDSM-werf**, a shipyard that now contains city-sponsored art studios. Grab a coffee at the sleek **IJ-kantine** right at the ferry pier, or the funkier **Noorderlicht**, inside the NDSM area.

Other highlights within the urban part of the Noord are the pretty homes and lush gardens that line **Stoombootweg**, on the west side, as well as **Nieuwendammerdijk** on the east, a beautiful long row of cottages with a village feel. Behind the dyke is **Nieuwendam**, an Amsterdam School housing project with winding streets and a pretty central square.

Heading north along the **Noordhollandsch Kanaal**, you'll pass a working windmill and soon be out in the country – a patchwork of fields divided by canals. You can make an easy loop around the villages of **Zunderdorp**, **Ransdorp**, **Holysloot** and **Broek in Waterland** (the last one's not technically in Amsterdam, but who's counting?). They're each only a few kilometres apart – though getting to or from Holysloot requires walking your bike across some fields and using the city's tiniest ferry.

Do pace yourself a bit as the wind is almost always against you when you turn back towards the city. If you time it right, you can finish up with dinner back at **Hotel de Goudfazant** in an industrial space directly on the IJ, and return to Centraal Station via the IJplein ferry.

INFORMATION

Location North across the IJ from Centraal Station; Broek in Waterland, the furthest village mentioned here, is 9km north

Getting there see ferry details on p174; Holysloot ferry (9.30am-5pm daily Jul-Aug, Sat & Sun only mid-Apr–May & Sep-Oct)

Eating IJ-kantine (☎ 633 71 62; www.ijkantine.nl; MT Ondinaweg 15-17; ☽ 9am-late); Noorderlicht (☎ 492 27 70; www.noorderlichtcafe.nl, in Dutch; TT Neveritaweg 33; ☽ 11am-late); Hotel de Goudfazant (☎ 636 15 70; www.hoteldegoudfazant.nl, in Dutch; Aambeeldstraat 10h; ☽ 6pm-1am Tue-Sun)

AMSTERDAMSE BOS

The Amsterdam Woods is a sprawling green area, roughly 2km by 5km of dense trees and open fields, cut through with cycling and walking paths. In the densest thickets you can forget you're near a city at all (until you hear the scud of a jet overhead on its way to nearby Schiphol), and it's a wonderful place to let kids run free.

The area was laid out during the 1930s as a make-work program, and it has grown up beautifully – rare birds nest in the grasslands, and frogs croak in the marshy areas. There's a botanical garden in an area called **Vogeleiland** (Bird Island), the reeds around the **Amsterdamse Poel** harbour wild orchids and you can go fishing in the lakes (get a permit at the visitors centre).

Take young ones to **De Ridammerhoeve**, a delightful working goat farm where kids can feed bottles of milk to, well, kids. The cafeteria sells tasty goat's-milk smoothies and ice cream, as well as cheeses made on the premises. Another converted old farmhouse, **Boerderij Meerzicht**, is a kid-friendly pancake restaurant.

On the north side, near the main entrance, the **Bosbaan** is a long lake for sculling – you can sit and watch the rowers from yet another cafe. Or you can rent a canoe yourself and paddle through some of the wetlands. Bicycles are available at the main entrance if you don't want to ride down on your own. And on Sundays during summer you can add yet another mode of transport to the trip: the Amsterdam Tram Museum runs vintage trams down to the south end of the Bos.

INFORMATION

Location 5.5km southwest of central Amsterdam
Getting there 🚌 170 or 172 from Centraal Station; tram from the Amsterdam Tram Museum (☎ 673 75 38; www.museumtram.nl; Amstelveenseweg 264; €4/2; 🕙 11am-5pm Sun Apr-Oct; 🚋 16); cycle through Vondelpark and due south on Amstelveenseweg (about 45min)
Contact visitors centre (☎ 545 61 00; www.amsterdamsebos.nl; Bosbaanweg 5)
Costs admission free; bicycles per hr/day €4.50/9; canoes per hr from €6
When to go visitors centre 🕙 noon-5pm, park 🕙 24hr
Eating De Ridammerhoeve (☎ 645 50 34; 🕙 10am-5pm Wed-Mon Mar-Oct, Wed-Sun Nov-Feb); Boerderij Meerzicht (☎ 679 27 44; Koenenkade 56; 🕙 11am-7pm Tue-Sun Mar-Oct, 10am-6pm Fri-Sun Nov-Feb)

Amsterdam's historic canal houses all look roughly the same on the outside. But inside there could be a jazz jam session, a gay club night, an intimate restaurant or a supercool hotel. Snapshots is a guide to which scenes flourish behind which canal-house doors.

When a herring craving strikes, head to one of the city's traditional herring stalls

ACCOMMODATION

Amsterdam is so compact that your hotel location doesn't matter a great deal – everything's relatively accessible. That said, you might prefer the character of a specific neighbourhood. The canal ring – any address on Herengracht, Keizersgracht, Prinsengracht or Singel – is the most desirable area, both for aesthetics and quiet. The **Hotel Pulitzer** (www.luxurycollection /pulitzer) is the loveliest, but you can get water views for less at **Prinsenhof** (www.hotelprinsenhof.com) and **Canal House** (www.canalhouse.nl), which will reopen after renovations in spring 2009. The Jordaan is charming, but has very few hotels – one is **Hotel van Onna** (www.hotelvanonna.nl). These areas also hold a lot of restaurants and cafes – it's easy to get home after a decadent dinner.

Unless you're not planning to actually sleep, we don't recommend staying in De Wallen (the red-light district) or anywhere on the Damrak, where the hotels are superficially decent but usually nasty inside. Better to stay a short walk away in the Nieuwmarkt area, at a place like **Misc Eat Drink Sleep** (www.hotelmisc.nl).

The area between Vondelpark and Museumplein – with midrange places like **Hotel Piet Hein** (www.hotelpiethein.nl) or **Hotel Fita** (www.hotelfita.com) – is handy for museum-goers, though not the liveliest at night. If you prefer to look at people rather than paintings, then multicultural De Pijp is the place to be – there aren't many hotels here, but places like **Between Art & Kitsch B&B** (www.between-art-and-kitsch.com) are relatively inexpensive.

Due to a shortage of hotel rooms, doing Amsterdam on the cheap can be impossible unless you plan months in advance. If only there were more places like the impeccable **Hotel Brouwer** (www.hotelbrouwer.nl), a lovely house in the Western Canal Belt. The hip **Lloyd Hotel** (www.lloydhotel.com) also has a few bargain rooms, though its Eastern Docklands location lacks much street life. Any cheaper, though, and you risk fleapit territory. Better opt for a hostel, like the high-style **Stayokay Zeeburg** (www.stayokay.com).

Expect to pay between €18 to €30 for a hostel bed, and anywhere from €80 to €300 for a double room during the summer high season. Except at the top end, you'll never get a lot of space, nor air-conditioning, and you'll probably have to carry your luggage up perilously steep stairs.

One of the great treats in Amsterdam is staying in some creatively adapted spaces. **Amrâth** (www.amrathamsterdam.com) occupies the stunning Scheepvaarthuis, **Hotel Arena** (www.hotelarena.nl) is a converted orphanage (and another good budget option), and the **Windketel** (www.windketel.nl), a bit west of the Jordaan, lets you sleep in a converted octagonal water tower.

For deals on some of these and larger hotels, visit www.hotels.nl. Or to really feel like a local, rent an apartment. **Citymundo** (www.citymundo.com) is a reliable broker, offering a range of great houseboats as well as studios and apartments for a minimum of three nights. You can also check www .expatica.com and www.craigslist.com for sublets, swaps and other options.

IF YOU LOVE...
> **Philosophy** Hotel de Filosoof (www .hotelfilosoof.nl)
> **Bikes** Bicycle Hotel Amsterdam (www.bicyclehotel.com)
> **Boats** Frederic's Houseboats (www .frederic.nl)
> **Bondage** Black Tulip (www.black tulip.nl)
> **Drop-dead luxury** Amstel (www .amsterdam.intercontinental.com)

TOP FIVE DESIGN HOTELS
> Amrâth (www.amrathamsterdam.com)
> Dylan (www.dylanamsterdam.com)
> Lloyd Hotel (www.lloydhotel.com)
> Lute Suites (www.lutesuites.com)
> Miauw Suites (www.miauw.com)

TOP FIVE CANAL VIEWS
> Canal House (www.canalhouse.nl)
> Hotel de L'Europe (www.leurope.nl)
> Pulitzer (www.luxurycollection .com/pulitzer)
> Seven Bridges (www.sevenbridges hotel.nl)
> Seven One Seven (www.717 hotel.nl)

TOP FIVE SMALL GEMS
> Brouwer (www.hotelbrouwer.nl)
> Collector (www.the-collector.nl)
> Maes B&B (www.bedandbreak fastamsterdam.com)
> Orlando (www.hotelorlando.nl)
> Xaviera Hollander B&B (www .xavierahollander.com)

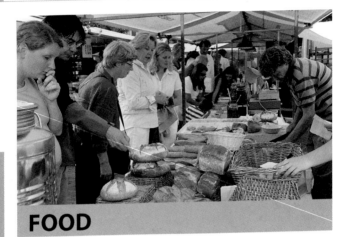

FOOD

Maybe it's the centuries of trade, maybe it's the meat-and-potatoes essence of traditional Dutch fare, but Amsterdammers embrace global cuisines with zeal. Even a humble *eetcafé* (a cafe that serves casual meals) might offer Indonesian satay, Moroccan couscous and Indian curry on its menu – all with a side of *frites* (French fries), of course. On any given night, you can eat Ethiopian, Thai or South African, but the most popular foreign cuisine is spicy Indonesian – the multiple-plate *rijsttafel* (rice table) is a Dutch invention.

The city's finer restaurants take inspiration from France, but they work with local produce, fish from the North Sea and lamb from the island of Texel. The result is uniquely Dutch – a potato salad with smoked eel at Greetje (p128) for instance, or a perfectly cooked piece of venison at Marius (p78). But as much as the Dutch mock their own cuisine, the places that stick to tradition can also be deeply satisfying. On a drizzly day, nothing hits the spot like a steak at Loetje (p101), or a big bowl of thick pea soup at Moeders (p70).

One distinct element of the Amsterdam dining scene is the large number of restaurants that serve only one or two set menus per night. Submitting to the whims of a chef can get you fresh-from-the-garden gourmet at De Kas (p117), international elegance at Gare de l'Est (p137) or casual camaraderie at Balthazar's Keuken (p68). Even restaurants that do a broader menu also offer one or two fixed-price three-course menus, which can be excellent value.

Dinner in Amsterdam can require a bit of planning. Aside from *eetcafés*, nearly every restaurant takes reservations, and any place with a bit of buzz will require a call at least a couple of days ahead. It never hurts to call a restaurant to reserve, even just a few hours early. Moreover, restaurants typically do only one seating per night. Amsterdammers dine relatively early, and once they sit down, they're at the table for the better part of the evening.

The midday meal, on the other hand, is usually a modest affair. The Dutch are quite fond of their cheese sandwiches, and haven't really taken to 'doing lunch'. There's no shortage of charming cafes in which to have a light bite, but some of the best bets are the spartan *broodje* (sandwich) shops like Van Dobben (p90) or Dop (p48) that serve white rolls with butter and thinly sliced meat.

Speaking of meat, vegetarians are generally well cared-for, with at least one meatless option on the menu just about anywhere you go. And there are a number of excellent all-vegetarian restaurants as well.

A note on service, an endless source of dismay for visitors and Dutch diners alike: yes, your waiter or waitress may often be distracted, or grumpy or forgetful. Just try to forget it and chalk it up to cultural difference – it's never personal. Etiquette demands that you must ask for your bill when you're ready to leave – the staff will never bring it unrequested, lest it appear they're trying to rush you.

BEST SWEET TREATS

> **Chocolate and cakes** Unlimited Delicious (p73)
> **Fancy lollies** Papabubble (p67)
> **Ice cream** IJscuypje (p110)
> **Stroopwafels** Lanskroon (p50)
> **Liquorice and more** Het Oude-Hollandsche Snoepwinkeltje (p66)

BEST BITES

> **Roast-beef sandwich** Van Dobben (p90)
> **Fries with Belgian mayo** Vlaams Frites Huis (p53)
> **Loempias** Albert Cuypmarkt (p106)
> **Fresh herring sandwich** Rob Wigboldus Vishandel (p51)
> **Aged gouda** De Kaaskamer (p69)

Top left Sample breads of the world at the Noordermarkt (p67) in the Jordaan

ARCHITECTURE

It's impossible not to be struck by Amsterdam's well-preserved beauty; the lovely canalscapes depicted in centuries-old paintings are remarkably unchanged. Historian Geert Mak once described Amsterdam as 'a Cinderella under glass', spared from wartime destruction and, for the most part, ham-fisted developers. The gracious old centre has no fewer than 7000 historical monuments, more humpback bridges than Venice and more trees per capita than Paris.

At first glance, the narrow buildings all look the same. But details like gables (decorations at roof-level) give clues to age: a simple pointed gable is the oldest, dating from the late 16th century, while steps ruled the 17th, and curvy bell gables were fashionable in the 18th.

You'll also notice that more recent constructions have been wedged in between these Golden Age relics. Many of the newer buildings – also brick, so they blend in – are from the early 20th century, in a style known as Amsterdam School (boxed text, p106). Visit masterpieces like the Scheepvaarthuis (p125), and also look at the canal bridges, especially along Leidsestraat, trimmed in winding wrought iron and odd animals. Even the shell-shaped green pissoirs around the city are Amsterdam School designs.

All the interesting new construction is on Amsterdam's fringes. Orient yourself first with a visit to the city planning exhibit at the Zuiderkerk (p125), then make the trek from the warren of the medieval centre out to the spacious Eastern Docklands (p132). Both areas have canals, but otherwise, they're worlds apart. In the harbour, the green ship-shaped NEMO (p133), built in 1997, is already a classic, while the 2007 OBA (Amsterdam Public Library; p136) next door redefines the public library. The Muziekgebouw (p139) is oriented purely towards the water. For even more inventive new building, visit the Bijlmer neighbourhood (p142), where architecture's effect on community is patently clear.

No matter what your architectural tastes, stop in at ARCAM (p133), the city architecture museum that is itself an ingenious structure. There's an excellent timeline showcasing the city's building history downstairs. The enthusiastic staff can recommend areas of the city to explore, and also run periodic tours around the city.

TOP ARCHITECTURAL ICONS
> Westerkerk (p63)
> Rijksmuseum (p98)
> NEMO (p133)
> Koninklijk Paleis (p42)
> Beurs van Berlage
  (p41)

TOP INTERIORS
> Tuschinskitheater
  (p85)
> Het Schip (p78)
> Museum Van Loon (p84)
> Rembrandthuis (p125)
> Oude Kerk (p43)

Above Set sail for one of Amsterdam's modern architectural icons, NEMO (p133), in the Eastern Docklands

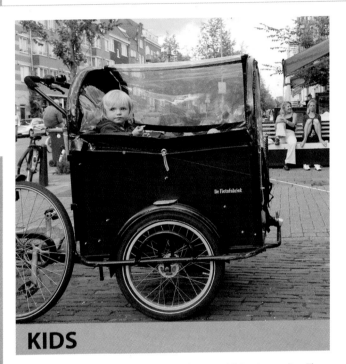

KIDS

Never mind the sex and drugs – Amsterdam is a children's paradise. The small scale, the quirky buildings, the lack of car traffic and the canals all combine to make it a wondrous place for little ones. And the Dutch seem to always be dreaming up new ways to entertain children. Whether that's a hands-on science museum like NEMO (p133), a free puppet show on Dam Square (p41) or simply a kid-oriented tour through the Rembrandthuis (p125) or Ons' Lieve Heer Op Solder (p42), the goal is to keep kids occupied and intrigued, so their parents can relax a little and enjoy themselves too. In fact, most of the major museums offer a kids' tour, and the Rijksmuseum (p98), is free for under-18s.

While you're at the NEMO (and you have to go, if only for the building – it's big and green and funny-looking, and the rooftop deck is a great spot for looking down on the city's medieval centre), be sure to visit the adjacent *Amsterdam* ship, with all its cubbyholes and a rambunctious, piratelike crew. Teens who've read *The Diary of Anne Frank* will certainly want to visit the Anne Frank Huis (p62), but if you need to entertain kids of all ages, the Tropenmuseum (p113) has enough colourful stuff from all over the world to impress everyone (including adults).

Kids often just need room to run around. That's easily found at Vondelpark (p99), in particular at Het Groot Melkhuis, a cafe adjoining a packed playground. Or make a day of it and head out to Amsterdamse Bos (p145) to the adorable goat farm where kids can feed and pet the animals.

Dining out is a little more limited – a lot of restaurants are quite small and quiet and have a romantic atmosphere. But anywhere that calls itself an *eetcafé* is casual enough not to mind smaller diners, and we especially recommend Loetje (p101), Bazar (p109) and Los Pilones (p70). Otherwise consider combining a free ferry ride with dinner at kid-friendly IJ-kantine at NDSM-werf (p144). In summertime, treat kids to *poffertjes* (mini-pancakes sprinkled with powdered sugar) at temporary stands (there's a circus-themed one just off the Leidseplein near Stadhouderskade); in winter, they're replaced with *oliebollen* (deep-fried proto-doughnuts). Little ones also love big Dutch-style pancakes – the tiny Pannenkoekenhuis Upstairs (p51) has a fairy-tale feel, and Pancakes! (p70) has a huge menu.

High-end hotels often offer baby-sitting services. To arrange your own, contact **Oppascentrale Kriterion** (Map pp122-3, D6; ☎ 624 58 48; www.kriterionoppas.org; Roetersstraat 170), the best known in town – but you need to register ahead of time and pay a nominal joining fee.

TOP KIDS' ACTIVITIES	TOP KIDS' SIGHTS
> Ice skating at Museumplein (p96)	> Amsterdamse Bos (p145)
> Canal-boat rides (p178)	> Artis Zoo (p121)
> Ferry across the IJ (p174)	> NEMO (p133)
> Eating pancakes (p70)	> Tropenmuseum (p113)
> TunFun (p131)	> Vondelpark (p99)

Top left A small child takes in the city's atmosphere from the comfort of its Bakfiets (p107)

SHOPPING

Amsterdam is filled with tiny speciality shops that seem to exist outside the laws of supply and demand. Shops stocked with nothing but buttons, beads or bowties may not be for you, but at some point, you'll turn a corner and see the store that specialises in precisely the thing you've been hunting for – whether you knew it or not.

Each neighbourhood has a different consumer character. In the Centrum, the long pedestrian strip formed by Kalverstraat and Nieuwendijk (Map pp38–9, B8-D3) has more H&M branches than you can count, plus there are large bookstores on the Spui. Over in De Wallen, the displays in the sex shops can cause serious whiplash. But just where the glow from the red lights fades, the Zeedijk (Map pp38–9, E4) has a string of lovely boutiques, alternating with long-established bars and Chinese groceries, and Oude Hoogstraat and Nieuwe Hoogstraat (Map pp38–9, D6-E6) offer another strip of eclectic shops.

Over in the Western Canal Belt, the Negen Straatjes (p14) are ground zero for quirky shopkeepers, but don't blow your budget before poking around other side streets here and in the neighbouring Jordaan. The Jordaan is known for its vintage goodies – but don't assume dust and clutter mean bargains. Centuries of savvy trading have made this city great, so you can bet the proprietor knows the value of a good piece of Bakelite.

There's less dust and far more valuable stuff in the Spiegelkwartier antiques district, the area along Spiegelgracht and Nieuwe Spiegelstraat in the Southern Canal Belt (Map pp82–3, C4). If you need the perfect 18th-century *objet* for the mantel in your country estate, come here first.

The city's modern luxury shopping street is Pieter Cornelisz Hooftstraat (Map p97, E2), with the obligatory Dolce & Gabbana and the like. Even if you're not in the market for a Vuitton bag, this street is interesting from an anthropological perspective: conspicuous consumption is generally frowned upon in Amsterdam, and these are the only few blocks where it appears to flourish. More genteel shoppers in the Old South head to pretty Cornelis Schuytstraat (Map p97, D3), off Vondelpark.

But once you find your dream item, be ready to pay cash – a surprising number of businesses don't take credit cards.

BEST HOUSEWARES
> Droog (p126)
> Frozen Fountain (p65)
> & Klevering (p64)
> Wonderwood (p47)
> HEMA (p45)

BEST FASHION
> Van Ravenstein (p68)
> Young Designers United (p86)
> Marlies Dekkers (p100)
> Hester van Eeghen (p65)
> Sprmrkt (p68)

BEST GIFTS
> **Custom shirt** Your Cup of T (p68)
> **Chocolates** Unlimited Delicious (p73)
> **Felt clogs** Shirdak (p67)
> **Bike seat cover** Kitsch Kitchen (p66)
> **Enamel zuiker (sugar) pot** De Emaillekeizer (p108)

BEST ANTIQUES & VINTAGE
> Waterloopleinmarkt (p127)
> Laura Dols (p67)
> De Looier (p65)
> Bebob Design (p85)
> Brilmuseum (p64)

Top left and **Above** Amsterdam's markets offer clothing, jewellery, food and almost everything in between

GAY & LESBIAN

To call Amsterdam a gay capital still doesn't express just how welcoming and open the scene is here. After all, this is the city that gave the world *Butt* magazine. It's also the city that claims to have founded the world's first gay and lesbian bar, 't Mandje (p56) – an obligatory stop on any Zeedijk cruise. It's also the city that hosts one of the world's largest and most flamboyant Pride parades, and certainly the only one that takes place on boats (p24).

Amsterdam's gay scene is a diverse one, with the Warmoesstraat perhaps the most notorious district, known for its numerous leather bars and darkrooms. Reguliersdwarsstraat is the polar opposite, all air-kissing and tight T-shirts – but there's plenty of action here too. Lesbians aren't quite so visible, but have several excellent bars to choose from – Vivelavie (p91) probably has the hottest crowd. The younger gay and lesbian subculture is more mixed, as at the come-one-come-all Getto (p54) in De Wallen, and the volunteer-run Sunday party at **De Trut** (Bilderdijkstraat 165e; admission €3; 🕙 11pm-4am Sun) – arrive early and be prepared to prove you're a *pot* (dyke) or a *flikker* (fag).

For more info – and the lowdown on many more gay and lesbian hangouts than this book can cover – visit the **Pink Point** (Map pp60-1, D5; 🕙 noon-6pm Mar-Aug, limited hours Sep-Feb) on the Keizersgracht, behind the Westerkerk. Part information kiosk, part souvenir shop, it's a good place to get details on parties and social groups, and pick up a copy of the very candid *Bent Guide*.

MUSEUMS

Amsterdam's Rembrandt-crammed Rijksmuseum (p98) is currently only partially open while it undergoes renovations, but consider it a blessing in disguise: your time is freed up to visit all the other beautiful, intimate and sometimes odd collections in town. Naturally, there's that collection of work by the Netherlands' *other* famous painter, the Van Gogh Museum (p98), as well as a token hash museum (p42) and a sex museum (p43).

Some grand canal houses are dedicated to some very special interests, such as the Bijbels Museum (p62), where you can see a hand-carved scale model of the Ark of the Covenant and other 19th-century oddities, and the Tassenmuseum Hendrikje (p85), a temple of handbags. A smaller waterside house contains Ons' Lieve Heer op Solder (p42), a Catholic church hidden in the upper floors, complete with an organ, while the luxurious yet cosy Museum Van Loon (p84) feels like the inhabitants just stepped out.

But visiting museums doesn't mean you'll be poking around in dusty old rooms full of artefacts. Both the Amsterdams Historisch Museum (p40) and the Verzetsmuseum (p125), which focus on the Resistance in WWII, use sound and video clips to great effect. The massive Tropenmuseum (p113), is an utterly absorbing tour of the Netherlands' former colonies and beyond. At the Rembrandthuis (p125) staff demonstrate crafts and printmaking techniques, and on the *Amsterdam* ship, moored next to NEMO (p133), scruffy sailors sing sea chanteys. The ship actually belongs to the Scheepvaartmuseum (p133), another collection that will probably be closed while you're here. But don't worry – with all the other museums to see, you'll never miss this one.

The Stedelijk Museum (p98), located in the centre of Amsterdam's museum district

GEZELLIGHEID

This particularly Dutch quality is one of the best reasons to visit Amsterdam. It's variously translated as snug, friendly, cosy, informal, companionable and convivial, but *gezelligheid* – the state of being *gezellig* – is something more easily experienced than defined. There's a sense of time stopping, an intimacy of the here and now that leaves all your troubles behind, at least until tomorrow.

You can get that warm, fuzzy feeling in many situations, but the easiest place is at a traditional *bruin café*. So-called 'brown cafes', covered in wood panelling and stained with centuries of tobacco smoke, practically have *gezelligheid* on tap, alongside the usual beer. (And why *are* the beer glasses so small here? You guessed it: more *gezellig*.) There's usually a reading table strewn with newspapers, where a couple of regulars sip their coffee and occasionally debate the issues. If the cafe cat strolls by and wants to be scratched, so much the better. By night, the golden lights come on and the beer flows freely. The oldest-school *bruin cafés* have no music, and encourage customers to toss their peanut shells on the floor.

You can also get into the *gezellig* mood at airier cafes with a pretty view, or any restaurant after dinner, where you're welcome to lounge and chat after your meal (*natafelen*, or, in Dutch, 'after-table-ing') while the candles burn low – and there are *always* candles.

Identifying the most *gezellig* spots seems a little too arbitrary – but these are some spots where we know *gezelligheid* can be found.

GEZELLIG BARS
> De Zotte (p74)
> Heuvel (p91)
> 't Mandje (p56)
> 't Smalle (p76)
> Welling (p102)

GEZELLIG CAFES & RESTAURANTS
> De Jaren (p47)
> Festina Lente (p70)
> Kapitein Zeppo's (p50)
> Latei (p55)
> Van Kerkwijk (p52)

SMOKING

Even for those who don't smoke marijuana, Amsterdam's capitalist approach to soft drugs is fascinating. 'Coffeeshops' sell pre-rolled joints in handy plastic cases, and their menus are as detailed as the best wine lists. 'Smart shops' deal in organic uppers and natural hallucinogens: fresh psychedelic mushrooms fill glass-front refrigerators, as at a gourmet grocery.

Skip the generic coffeeshops with the *Pulp Fiction* soundtrack on repeat and head instead to one of the mosaic-bedecked branches of the Greenhouse (p111). Newbies will like friendly Abraxas (p53), minimalist Kadinsky (p55) is for nonhippy smokers, La Tertulia is wholesome (p75), and Rokerij (p91) is a feast for the eyes. Or you could pop into a random coffeeshop in a residential neighbourhood – usually generic, but barely distinguishable from a corner bar.

A good budtender can suggest a smoke for your tastes and won't make you buy more than a gram of anything. You're not obliged to buy weed to sit in a coffeeshop and smoke, but do pick something from the menu – nice places have all kinds of stoner-friendly treats. They'll also have pipes, bongs and vaporisers you can use.

Etiquette demands that you smoke only in coffeeshops or weed-friendly bars (the latter are rarer than you think). But thanks to a 2008 cigarette ban, if you want to mix tobacco and THC, a secluded corner of a park is your only option (for more on the no-tobacco policy, see boxed text, p55). Obligatory warnings: marijuana is strong here, probably stronger than you've ever smoked, so start slow. And please listen to the expert folks who sell magic mushrooms. Every year, the city considers banning them, due to another case of a tourist who consumed too many. Don't be the person who ruins it for everyone.

The grass is always greener in Amsterdam

SNAPSHOTS

DRINKING & NIGHTLIFE

Though it has a wanton reputation, Amsterdam is not an all-night city, and in fact some of the most delightful drinking options – such as Brouwerij 't IJ (p129) and Wijnand Fockink (p56) – kick you out just as the sun is setting. But that doesn't mean Amsterdammers don't know how to party.

That party starts at all manner of bars: *gezellig* brown cafes (p160), chic lounges where DJs spin (cocktails are rare though) or specialists in Belgian beer. Visit sedate *proeflokalen* (tasting houses) for *jenever* (Dutch-style gin) and flavoured liqueurs, usually distilled on the premises. They're served in fluted glasses filled to the brim – bend over and slurp your first taste.

The club scene is massive – Holland gave the world Tiësto and gabber, after all. International names drop in all the time and there are extended parties like 5 Days Off (p23) and Amsterdam Dance Event (p25). At the city's many casual clubs, it really *is* all about the music – velvet ropes and VIP rooms are relatively rare. Check out record shops for party flyers and ticket presales.

The city's numerous multipurpose arts centres are one of its finest assets. At places like the Melkweg (p93), Studio K (p118) and De Badcuyp (p111), you can eat a meal, see a movie, hear a band and probably see some art on the walls. And once the bands stop, club music takes over. Funkier squats (many now legalised) such as OT301 (p103) and Zaal 100 (p75) have an even more freewheeling agenda.

BEST BARS FOR...
> **A view** Canvas op de 7e (p118)
> **An eclectic crowd** Het Schuim (p54)
> **Belgian beer** De Zotte (p74)
> **Cheap beer** Vrankrijk (p56)
> **Jenever** Wijnand Fockink (p56)

BEST CLUBS
> Club 8 (p75)
> Escape (p92)
> Paradiso (p94)
> Studio K (p118)
> Sugar Factory (p95)

MULTICULTURALISM

Scratch that vision of a metropolis of 6ft-tall blond people. With nearly half of its population hailing from other countries, Amsterdam rivals much bigger cities for diversity. People from the Netherlands' former colonies, Indonesia and Suriname, form the largest minority groups, and the other significant presences in the city are Turks and Moroccans, many second-generation. The remaining 170 or so nationalities recorded in the census represent the rest of the globe.

Amsterdam has its share of racial and cultural issues (which came to a head in 2004, when filmmaker Theo van Gogh was murdered by a young Dutch-Moroccan), but it is remarkably integrated compared with some other European capitals. Immigrants aren't relegated to suburbs (just walk around De Pijp to hear five or 10 languages spoken), and pop Dutch movies like *Shouf Shouf Habibi* (p171) pack in the crowds. Amsterdam's multiracial character is a point of pride and, post-Theo, many Amsterdammers have scoffed at nationalist politicians such as MP Geert Wilders, the firebrand who likened the Quran to *Mein Kampf*.

And Amsterdammers always seem ready to bond over commerce – the wildly diverse Albert Cuypmarkt (p106) and Dappermarkt (p113) are two fantastic places to see this in action. For a deeper tour of Amsterdam's immigrant heritage, make a trip to the Bijlmer (p142), a housing project with a rich past. Then check out what's on at multicultural venues like De Badcuyp (p111) or Podium Mozaïek (see boxed text, p75) to hear what Amsterdam's future will sound like.

MUSIC

Amsterdam fosters music geeks. Similar to the city's niche shops, there's a fervent subculture for just about every genre – just hang out near your favourite albums at Concerto (p85) and you'll soon be swapping trivia with fellow fans. There's a particularly hot avant-garde improvisational music scene in small venues like Zaal 100 (boxed text, p75) and grand ones like Bimhuis (p139), a sleek new concert hall on the IJ that carries the spirit of a much older, funkier club inside it.

If that's too geeky for you, hit one of the more traditional jazz clubs. In the city where Chet Baker met his end, you can see a live combo every night of the week. Two stalwarts are Jazz Café Alto (p93), where fusion saxophonist Hans Dulfer takes to the stage every Wednesday, and De Engelbewaarder (p130), for its long-running Sunday session. Visiting musicians usually play at Bimhuis.

Classical fans will also be delighted by Amsterdam, with the flawless Concertgebouw (p102) or the dramatic Muziekgebouw aan 't IJ to choose from. Lunchtime concerts and student shows at the Conservatorium van Amsterdam (p139) are often free.

The city's dance music scene thrives as well, with DJs catering to nearly every taste – see Nightlife (p162) for club recommendations. Local rock doesn't have much notoriety beyond the now-deceased Herman Brood, who burned out rather than faded away, but huge touring names often play smallish venues like Melkweg (p93) and Paradiso (p94). It's a treat to catch one of your favourites here.

A local band offers a tune to the masses visiting the Noordermarket (p67)

The old and the new: traditional gables on the left, modern building by Mart van Schindel on the right

BACKGROUND

HISTORY

FROM THE BEGINNING

The region that spawned a giant trading community was originally an inhospitable patchwork of lakes, swamps and peat. The oldest archaeological finds here date from the Roman Empire, but the first settlement was not until around 1200, when a fishing community known as Aemstelredamme – 'the dam across the Amstel River' – emerged at what is now the Dam (p41). On 27 October 1275, the count of Holland (Holland being the name of the surrounding territory) waived tolls on locks and bridges for those who lived around the dam, and the town of Amsterdam was born.

EARLY TRADE

Although the earliest settlers focused on fishing, it was commercial trade – particularly in beer, an essential commodity at a time when water wasn't clean enough to drink – that soon put Holland on the map. Amsterdam muscled into the North and Baltic Seas, sending *vrijbuiters* (booty-chasers), with their holds full of cloth and salt to exchange for grain and timber, to crack the German Hanseatic League that ruled the trade routes. By the late 1400s, nearly two-thirds of ships sailing to and from the Baltic Sea were from Holland, and most were based in Amsterdam. The original harbour on the Damrak and Rokin was extended north into the IJ river, near what is now Centraal Station. Canals were dug to the warehouses in today's medieval centre. Unfettered by high taxes and medieval feudal structures, Amsterdam fostered a society of individualism and capitalism.

INDEPENDENT REPUBLIC

The Protestant Reformation of the 15th century spawned a doctrine espoused by French theologian John Calvin. Stern and austere, Calvinism became an integral element in the struggle of the Low Countries (as Belgium, Luxembourg and the Netherlands were known) against the decadent Catholic reign of Spain's Philip II and the Inquisition. In 1578 Calvinists captured Amsterdam and soon declared the northern provinces the independent Dutch Republic of the Seven United Netherlands, with Holland (and Amsterdam) at its core. The Calvinist ascension was tactfully called the 'Alteration', and business carried on as usual.

GOLDEN AGE

When trading rival Antwerp was retaken by the Spaniards in the late 16th century, merchants, skippers and artisans flocked to Amsterdam, and a new moneyed society emerged. The world's first regular newspaper was printed here in 1618. Persecuted Jews from Portugal and Spain also fled to Amsterdam; they knew of trade routes to the West and East Indies, introduced the diamond industry and made Amsterdam a tobacco centre. Founded in 1602, the Vereenigde Oost-Indische Compagnie (VOC, or Dutch East India Company), wrested the Asian spice trade from the Portuguese and took hold of the islands that would later be called Indonesia. By the late 17th century, the VOC was the world's richest corporation, with more than 50,000 employees and a private army.

Meanwhile the city kept pace and the population quadrupled in just a century, to 220,000 in 1700. Amsterdam became home to Europe's largest ship-building industry and, as wages remained low, investment flowed in. A less profitable West India Company established plantations in South America and the trading post of New Amsterdam. In a 1651 deal with the British, the Dutch chose to keep Guyana (later Suriname), and give up its northern territory – the British renamed it New York. Two decades later, Louis XIV of France invaded the Low Countries, and the brief era known as the Dutch Golden Age ended.

DECLINING FORTUNES

By the late 17th century, Dutch merchants began to invest their fortunes in secure ventures, rather than daring sea voyages and innovation. The result was stagnation, and the decline in trade brought poverty; exceptionally cold winters, especially in 1740 and 1763, froze supply boats in the river and led to serious food shortages. The mighty VOC went bankrupt in 1800, not long after the French revolutionary forces invaded the Dutch Republic. In 1806, it became a monarchy, an event soon followed by Napoleon Bonaparte's brother, Louis, occupying the city hall on the Dam with the declaration *Ik ben u konijn!* (I am your rabbit!) – he'd meant to say *koning* (king). Napoleon soon dismissed him and annexed the region into the French Empire. Amsterdam's great trade and fishing industries ground to a halt, and the city lapsed into a sleepy market town. Napoleon was defeated in 1813, opening the door for the House of Orange-Nassau to establish the United Kingdom of the Netherlands. But Amsterdam's trade with the world recovered slowly – the British had since come to dominate the seas.

GROWTH & DEPRESSION

Amsterdam shook off its torpor when the Netherlands' first rail line was inaugurated here in 1839. Major infrastructure projects such as an expanded harbour helped the city benefit from the Industrial Revolution. As the city again attracted immigrants, speculators hastily erected tenement blocks. In 1889, Centraal Station was built, its position on the IJ symbolically severing Amsterdam's historical ties with the sea. The Netherlands remained neutral in WWI, but Amsterdam's trade with the East Indies suffered because of naval blockades. Following riots over food shortages, an attempt to bring the socialist revolution to the Netherlands was halted by loyalist troops.

After the war the Netherlands focused on rebuilding its industrial base, with rapid success. Amsterdam's NDSM (Dutch Dock and Shipbuilding Company) operated the world's second-largest wharf. KLM (Royal Aviation Company) began the world's first regular air service in 1920 between Amsterdam and London, from an airstrip south of the city, and bought many of its planes from the factory of aviation pioneer Anthony Fokker to the north of the IJ. There were two huge breweries, a sizeable clothing industry and even a local car factory, and the city hosted the Olympic Games in 1928. But the global Depression of the 1930s hit Amsterdam hard. Make-work projects did little to defuse the mounting tensions between socialists, communists and a small but vocal fascist party.

WWII

When Germany invaded the Netherlands in May 1940, Amsterdammers experienced war first-hand for the first time in almost 400 years. In February 1941, dockworkers led a protest strike over the treatment of Jews. But it was already too late. Of Amsterdam's 90,000 Jews, only 5,000 survived the war, the lowest proportion of anywhere in Western Europe. Canadian troops liberated the city in May 1945, but not before thousands of people had starved or frozen to death in the previous months, known as the 'Hunger Winter'.

POSTWAR CHANGE

Shortly after the war, Indonesia gained independence. US aid and newly discovered natural-gas fields helped make up for lost profits during the war years, and the city began to grow again. Massive apartment blocks were constructed to meet the continued demand for housing. By the 1960s, these were often reserved for 'guest workers' from Morocco and Turkey, who filled jobs in the industrial sectors.

By the end of the '60s, Amsterdam became Europe's 'Magic Centre': hippies smoked dope on the Dam, camped in Vondelpark and tripped at clubs like the Melkweg, an abandoned dairy barn. In 1972 the first coffeeshop opened and in 1976 marijuana was decriminalised, to free up police resources for combating hard drugs. With soaring housing prices, squatters began to occupy buildings left empty by speculators; in the process, they helped save several notable historic structures from demolition. Historic preservation became a citywide issue in the early 1980s, when plans for a metro line and city hall complex in the old Jewish neighbourhood brought protesters to the streets.

AMSTERDAM TODAY

Since the 1990s, squatting has become more subdued and the city's economy has shifted to white-collar jobs, a thriving service industry and increasing gentrification. The ethnic make-up has changed too, with non-Dutch nationalities comprising over 45% of the population. In the first years of the 21st century, a noisy debate erupted over the Netherlands' policy towards migrants. Right-wing MP candidate Pim Fortuyn transfixed the country in 2002 when he declared the country 'full', then died from an assassin's bullet before elections. His killer wasn't one of the Muslims he'd condemned for homophobia, but an animal-rights activist angered by his stance on mink farming. In the autumn of 2004, outspoken filmmaker Theo van Gogh, also known for his anti-Islamic views, was shot and stabbed to death on an Amsterdam street. The killer was a young Muslim, born and raised in the Netherlands. The government swiftly mounted a unity campaign called 'We Amsterdammers', which appears to have pulled the populace together. After some stressful years, city residents have recently turned their attention to a new metro line, massive artificial suburban islands and other grand urban projects. According to local polls, for the first time in years the majority of Amsterdam's residents are happy with their jobs and have cause for optimism.

LIFE AS AN AMSTERDAMMER

Freewheeling Amsterdam is often praised for its tolerance and open-mindedness. Soft drugs, sex, nudity, eccentric behaviour – it's all met with a wry smile and a shrug, a blasé attitude developed over centuries of seeing the world flow in and out of this trading port. In fact, many *mokums* (slang for Amsterdam natives, from the Yiddish name for the city, Groot Mokum) are not just tolerant, but actively proud of the red-light district and the blatant mix of sex and industry that it represents. Gay marriage (legalised in 2001) and doctor-assisted suicide (euthanasia; permitted since 1993) are treated with the same approach. The old Calvinist streak comes out only in a dislike of attention-seeking behaviour: 'Act normal – that's crazy enough' is a common expression.

Some visitors think this means that Amsterdam is a nonstop drug-fuelled orgy. If anything, it's a nonstop *koffie verkeerd* (milky coffee) on a sunny terrace while chatting with a friend. A typical Amsterdammer has never set foot in a coffeeshop, and if they've tried marijuana, it was probably while they were on holiday in Australia. As for the red-light district, the city estimates that only 5% of customers are Dutch nationals.

Likewise, many Dutch people don't care much about the impression they make – at least beyond the polite routine of three cheek-kisses. They dress casually and comfortably (all the better for bicycling). They push to the head of the queue. And they speak their minds, often to the point of being shockingly blunt.

The cherished Dutch tolerance has also revealed its negative side. Tolerating something is in fact quite different from accepting it, say young people of Moroccan and Turkish descent. Though they're native-born citizens of the Netherlands, some ethnic Dutch still dismiss them as *allochtonen* ('out-landers'). Following some uncharacteristically divisive political debate, the Netherlands seems to be growing more conservative, favouring a Christian coalition government, restricting immigration and casting a critical eye. But this city of roughly 750,000 has largely remained staunchly left wing, looking instead to the needs of its own diverse citizens, 28% of whom are second-generation immigrants. At the heart of it, this is another element of their city that Amsterdammers are – and always will be – very proud of.

FURTHER READING

The most accessible and entertaining history of the city is *Amsterdam: A Brief Life of the City,* by Geert Mak. It combines broad historical narrative with anecdotes about Amsterdam's more riveting characters over the centuries. Mak, one of the country's leading journalists, does not shy away from depicting uncomfortable truths, be it in trade, war, religion or government. Another excellent history is Simon Schama's *The Embarrassment of*

Riches, an account of Dutch culture in the Golden Age. Schama also ties the Calvinist culture to modern Dutch society, and often turns to analysis of art – you'll learn a lot about breakfast paintings – to mirror a nation with all its neuroses and religious idiosyncrasies. Ian Buruma's *Murder in Amsterdam: Liberal Europe, Islam and the Limits of Tolerance* is a rather personal approach to the immigration debates and the death of Theo van Gogh, whom Buruma knew well.

Little Dutch fiction has made it into English, with the exception of Harry Mulisch's *De Aanslag* (The Assault), a devastating novel linking the tragedies of WWII with Cold War–era nuclear fears. Mulisch's rival, Amsterdam-born Gerard Reve, was notorious for his depiction of gay sex, often with caustic humour, and he never met a religious symbol that he didn't desecrate. None of his work is translated but his novel *De Vierde Man* (The Fourth Man) was made into a film by Paul Verhoeven in 1983.

On a more practical note, if you're a food fan, pick up a copy of Johannes van Dam's *Delicious Amsterdam*, a list of a hundred recommended restaurants (not entirely up-to-date) and a handy list of Dutch food words, for maximising your bakery time.

FILMS

Check out these films for insights into Dutch society – and scenic shots of Amsterdam. (We're specifically not recommending *Amsterdamned*, the silly 1987 thriller – the canal chase scenes were shot in Utrecht!).

De Aanslag (The Assault; 1986; Fons Rademakers). A physician spends his adult life investigating why his neighbours betrayed his family in WWII. Based on a best-selling novel by Harry Mulisch (above) and nominated for an Academy Award.

Interview (2003; Theo van Gogh). One of Van Gogh's more subdued films, in which a war correspondent conducts an interview with a soap-opera actress. An American remake was released in 2007.

Shouf Shouf Habibi (Hush Hush Baby; 2004; Albert ter Heerdt). A comedy about a Moroccan family finding its way in Dutch society, which takes a cynical look at the integration issue without taking sides.

Simon (2004; Eddy Terstall). A complicated friendship develops when a hetero hash dealer hits a gay man with his car. Simon is a pitch-perfect old-guard Jordaan native, and the film hits all the major social debates – drugs, gay rights, euthanasia – with humour.

Zus & So (2001; Paula van der Oest). A comedy about three sisters who plot to sabotage the engagement of their gay brother for material gain. Also Oscar-nominated.

Zwartboek (Black Book; 2006; Paul Verhoeven). This action-packed story explores some of the less heroic aspects of the Dutch resistance in WWII. The highest-grossing film in Dutch history, it launched the international career of today's hottest Dutch actress, Carice van Houten.

DIRECTORY
TRANSPORT
ARRIVAL & DEPARTURE

AIR
Amsterdam's **Schiphol International Airport** (☎ 794 08 00; www.schiphol.nl), 18km southwest of the city centre, is Europe's fourth-largest airport. There's a left-luggage office as well as lockers, which start at €5 per day. No matter where you arrive, you'll be funnelled into Schiphol Plaza, a shopping area that surrounds the train station.

TRAIN
National and international trains arrive at Amsterdam Centraal Station (Map pp38–9, E2). Trains run every 20 minutes from Rotterdam (1 hour) and Den Haag (1 hour). From Berlin, there's one direct day train (6 hours) and one night train (9 hours), plus connect-ing services. Six daily trains run from Frankfurt (4 hours). If you're coming from Hamburg, you must transfer in Hannover. The high-speed Thalys runs from Paris (4.5 hours) via Brussels nearly every 30 minutes between 6am and 9pm. Coming from London (5.5–7 hours) on the Eurostar requires a transfer in Brussels; there are seven departures daily, but only five onward connecting trains (one extra on weekends).

See www.ns.nl for national schedules and booking; www.nshispeed.nl for international booking; www.thalys.com for Paris and Brussels; www.eurostar.com for London.

BUS
Eurolines (www.eurolines.com) connects Amsterdam with all major European capitals. Buses arrive at Amstelstation, south of the centre, with an easy metro link to Centraal Station.

CLIMATE CHANGE & TRAVEL
Travel – especially air travel – is a significant contributor to global climate change. At Lonely Planet, we believe that all who travel have a responsibility to limit their personal impact. As a result, we have teamed with Rough Guides and other concerned industry partners to sup-port Climate Care, which allows people to offset the greenhouse gases they are responsible for with contributions to energy-saving projects and other climate-friendly initiatives in the developing world. Lonely Planet offsets all staff and author travel.

For more information, turn to the responsible travel pages on www.lonelyplanet.com. For details on offsetting your carbon emissions and a carbon calculator, go to www.climatecare.org.

GETTING INTO TOWN

Train

From 6am to midnight, trains run to and from Amsterdam Centraal Station (Map pp38–9, E2) every 15 minutes. The service takes 20 minutes and costs €3.80. If you have coins, buy tickets from the machines; if not, you must purchase at the window for a €0.50 surcharge.

Bus

Connexion (☎ 038-339 47 41; www.airporthotelshuttle.nl; one-way/return €13.50/22) drops you at your hotel door. Departures are every 30 minutes from 6am to 9pm; look for the desk by Arrivals 4.

Taxi

A taxi to the city centre takes 20 to 30 minutes (longer in rush hour) and costs €40 to €45. Shared taxis start at €21, and must be booked ahead at www.schiphol.nl.

FERRY

From London, **Stena Line** (www.stena line.co.uk) runs a service that includes the ferry between Harwich and Hoek van Holland, plus connecting rail service on either end. Total travel time is 13 hours during the day and 12 hours for the night trip.

CAR

It is most convenient to leave your car in a park-and-ride lot near the edge of town. A nominal parking fee also gets you free bicycles or public transport tickets. For more info see www.bereikbaaramster dam.nl.

GETTING AROUND

Central Amsterdam is relatively compact and best seen on foot or by bicycle. The public transport system is a mix of tram, metro and bus, operated by the **Gemeente Vervoerbedrijf** (GVB; www.gvb.nl). Visitors will use only the trams, except in a few cases. This book notes the nearest tram/metro/bus stop after the 🚊 / M / 🚌 icon in each listing.

The excellent website www.9292ov.nl calculates routes, costs and travel times. It's only in Dutch – enter your street address, and 'Amsterdam' in the Plaats line.

At press time, the Netherlands was in the process of switching from paper *strippenkaarten* (strip tickets; see boxed text p175) to a pass card called the *OV-chipkaart*. Using this card, journeys will be charged at a flat fee per boarding, plus a per-kilometre rate. Tram conductors and GVB vending

RAIL EASY TRAVEL

Amsterdam has very convenient train connections with other European capitals. Budget airfares may look tempting, but given odd flight times, out-of-the-way airports and perhaps a taxi fare to the airport, the train is often much handier and occasionally even cheaper. New high-speed tracks between Amsterdam and the Belgian border are set for completion in early 2009, making the trip from southern points even more efficient. Consider extending your trip with an extra day in Brussels or Paris – as easy as hopping off and hopping back on.

machines sell single-ride passes (€2.50), but repeat or long-stay visitors can invest in a *chipkaart* for €7.50, valid for five years; you can add up to €30 in credit at a time, and rides are cheaper.

Centraal Station, where most visitors arrive, is under construction for the foreseeable future, and tram depots have been relocated. For trams 4, 9, 16, 24 and 25, head far to the left (east) when you come out the front of the station.

TRAM, METRO, BUS & NIGHT BUS

Fast, frequent trams operate between 6am and 12.30am. Conductors work on most trams, but it's a good idea to buy an *OV-chipkaart* (opposite) beforehand. On trams with conductors, enter through the next-to-last door; when you enter and exit, wave your pass card over the sensors.

The metro and buses serve primarily outer districts. The small Stop/Go bus runs from Waterlooplein (Map pp122–3, B4) to Oosterdok (Map pp134–5, A4) and the harbour via Prinsengracht between 9am and 5.30pm; flag it down, as there are no fixed stops. *Nachtbussen* (night buses) run after other transport stops, between 1am and 6am. The routes radiate out from Centraal Station, with service roughly every hour.

TRAVEL PASSES

The GVB offers passes for 24/48/72/96 hours (€7/11.50/14.50/17.50), available at VVV offices (p179), metro-station machines (up to 72 hours only) and tram conductors (24 hours only). The All in Travel Ticket (per 24/48/72/96hr €12.95/17/19.70/22.40) includes the round-trip fare from Schiphol; get it at the Holland Tourism desk at the airport. The I amsterdam Card (p176) also includes a travel pass.

FERRY

Free ferries run to Amsterdam-Noord, departing from piers behind Centraal Station. The ride to Buiksloterweg is the most direct (five minutes) and runs 24 hours.

Another boat runs to NDSM-werf (15 minutes) between 7am and midnight (1am on Saturday), and another goes to IJplein (6.30am to midnight). Bicycles are permitted.

BICYCLE

Many visitors rent a bike towards the end of their stay and wish they had done so sooner. We can't recommend it highly enough. Rental companies can be found all over town; all require ID plus a cash deposit or credit-card imprint. Most have a variety of bicycles, starting with single-speed models with coaster brakes; handbrakes and gears cost a little more. Handy to Centraal Station is **Holland Rent-a-Bike** (Map pp38-9, C4; ☎ 622 32 07; Damrak 247; per 24hr €15) in the Beurs van Berlage (p41). **Bike City** (Map pp60-1, C5; ☎ 626 37 21; www.bikecity .nl; Bloemgracht 68-70; per 24hr €14.50) puts no advertising on its bikes, so you can pretend you're a local.

For route planning, visit www .routecraft.nl, which calculates best bike paths; click on 'Bikeplanner' for (mostly) English.

TAXI

Find taxis at stands at Centraal Station (Map pp38–9, E2), Leidseplein (Map pp82–3, A4) and a few hotels, or call one; **Taxicentrale Amsterdam** (TCA; ☎ 777 77 77) is the most reliable. Rates are roughly €3.40 plus €1.94 per kilometre – a ride from the Leidseplein to the Dam runs about €12. Drivers sometimes cannot change large bills (or claim they can't) and often don't know smaller streets. At taxi stands look for a pink ID card displayed in the window, which allows drivers to drive on tram lines, and shows the driver has passed a city knowledge exam; you needn't take the first car in the queue. Late at night, it's sometimes possible to negotiate a flat rate before starting out.

A nice alternative when available, motorised **tuk-tuks** (☎ 0900 993 33 99; www.tuktukcompany.nl, in Dutch) and yellow **bicycle taxis** (www.fiets taxiamsterdam.nl, in Dutch) often have lower rates, and can be flagged down in the street.

PRACTICALITIES

BUSINESS HOURS

Government offices and banks open from 9am to 5pm Monday to Friday. Most shops open at 10am or 11am to 6pm, but open a couple of hours later on Monday mornings. They're either closed on Sundays or open for a few hours, but often stay open a couple of hours later on Thursday nights. Grocery stores are usually open until at least 8pm. Restaurants serving lunch open at 11am; for dinner they open at 6pm. Though many restaurants stay open until midnight, their kitchens usually shut by 10pm. Very few restaurants are open specifically for breakfast; some cafes open at 9am or earlier, but 10am is more common. Many restaurants are shut on Sunday and/or Monday. Cafes and most bars are open until 1am on weekdays, and 3am on weekends; a few *nachtbars* (night bars) open and close two hours later. Clubs close at 4am or 5am. Almost all museums close by 5pm.

DISCOUNTS

Seniors over 65 (and their partners 60 or older) get reductions on public transport, museums, concerts and more. People under 30 can purchase the **Cultureel Jongeren Paspoort** (Cultural Youth Passport; www.cjp.nl; €15) for big discounts at museums and cultural events. Eve-

ryone's eligible for the **I amsterdam Card** (www.iamsterdam.com; per 24/36/72hr €33/43/53), which gives free admission to most museums, canal boat trips, and assorted discounts and freebies and includes a GVB transit pass. The **Museumkaart** (www .museumkaart.nl, in Dutch; adult/under 24yr €35/17.50) is valid for a year and grants free admission to 30 museums in Amsterdam; buy it at the Uitburo (boxed text, p93).

ELECTRICITY

The standard voltage throughout the Netherlands is 220V, 50Hz. Plugs are of the continental Europe two-round-pin variety.

EMERGENCIES

In a life-threatening emergency, the EU-wide telephone number for an ambulance, police and fire brigade is ☎ 112. For nonemergency police help, call ☎ 0900 88 44. For nonemergency medical care out of business hours, call ☎ 088-003 06 00, and have your postcode ready; you'll be directed to the nearest hospital, which will have a doctor waiting.

HOLIDAYS

Nieuwjaarsdag New Year's Day, 1 January.
Pasen (Easter) Goede Vrijdag (Good Friday); Eerste and Tweede Paasdag (Easter Sunday and Easter Monday), late March/early April.
Koninginnedag Queen's Day, 30 April.
Bevrijdingsdag Liberation Day, 5 May.

Hemelvaartsdag Ascension Day, 21 May 2009 and 13 May 2010.
Eerste and Tweede Pinksterdag Whit Sunday (Pentecost) and Whit Monday, 31 May and 1 June 2009, 23 and 24 May 2010.
Eerste and Tweede Kerstdag Christmas Day and Boxing Day, 25 & 26 December.

Additionally, many restaurants and other businesses close for two to six weeks in summer, usually in July or early August.

INTERNET

Dedicated internet cafes are not common, but the lovely public library (p136) has plenty of free terminals, and many coffeeshops have a computer or two. Wi-fi is prevalent. Useful websites include:
Backpackers on High Heels (www.bon highheels.com) Hip local girls give good shopping tips.
Eastern Docklands Amsterdam (www.easterndocklands.com) Suggested bike and walking tours of the area.
I amsterdam (www.iamsterdam.nl) Official city tourism info, well presented – look for special tips from 'I ambassadors'.
Le cool (www.lecool.com) Weekly email with tips on parties, art and more.
NL Streets (www.nlstreets.nl) A cool scrolling interface leads you through Amsterdam's best shopping quarters.
SpecialBite (www.specialbite.com) What's new and cool on the dining scene.
Spotted by Locals (http://amsterdam.spottedbylocals.com) Good recommendations for cafes and other hangouts, but not updated very frequently.

MONEY

Though locals are still complaining about the euro changeover, Amsterdam is not as expensive as other major cities in Europe. Count on spending between €50 and €80 per day in addition to your lodging. Many restaurants offer good-value three-course set menus, and there are plenty of entertaining free things to do (p31). For currency exchange rates, see the inside front cover or www.xe.com.

A surprisingly large number of shops and restaurants do not accept credit cards, while travellers cheques can only be cashed at a handful of banks in the centre and are generally accompanied by exorbitant fees. ATMs are not hard to find, but often have queues; stock up when you think of it.

NEWSPAPERS

The major Amsterdam paper is the left-leaning *Het Parool;* national papers include sensationalist *De Telegraaf* and the high-toned *NRC Handelsblad.* The *International Herald Tribune* has an English language Dutch-news insert from *Het Financieele Dagblad. Amsterdam Weekly* is a free listings tabloid, which is also online at www.amsterdamweekly.com. *Dutch News* (www.dutchnews.nl) summarises daily headlines, and is available online only.

ORGANISED TOURS
WALKING TOURS

Although just walking around on your own is stunning enough, a guide can point out details and answer any nagging questions you may have. **Mee in Mokum** (☎ 625 13 90; www.gildeamsterdam.nl; €4) offers the cheapest and often the most intriguing tours, led by senior-citizen volunteers who often have personal recollections to add. Agency **Like-A-Local** (www.like-a-local .com) arranges tours, home visits and meals with Amsterdammers. Get the inside knowledge on art and architecture with tony **Artifex** (☎ 620 81 12; www.artifex-travel.nl, in Dutch), or more affordable **Urban Home & Garden Tours** (☎ 688 12 43; www.uhgt.nl; from €26.50). The Prostitution Information Centre (p43) covers lower-brow topics in De Wallen (the red-light district).

BOAT TOURS

By far the best option is **St Nicolaas Boat Club** (Map pp82-3, A3; www.amsterdam boatclub.com) and its small, open boats that can go into the narrowest canals. The captains are more entertaining too – and they only ask for a donation at the end; sign up at Boom Chicago (p92). If you *must* ride with the bigger boats (like, if it's raining), then **Meyers** (Map pp38-9, D3; ☎ 623 42 08; www.meyersrondvaarten.nl, in Dutch; Damrak 4; admission €7.50/3.75) is at

least the cheapest, and handily located just south of Centraal Station.

A great way to see old industry and new architecture on the IJ is on a boat operated by the **Amsterdam Public Transport Museum** (☎ 0900 423 11 00; www.museum-ijveren-amsterdam .nl, in Dutch; full/half tour €4.50/3, per bicycle €3). They run from pier 14 behind Centraal Station on Sundays only, from late March to late October; see the website for schedules.

TELEPHONE

The Netherlands uses GSM 900/1800 mobile (cell) phones, compatible with the rest of Europe and Australia but not with the North American GSM 1900 (some convertible phones work in both places). SIM cards start around €20, with €10 credit.

Coin-operated public phones have made a comeback, but many still take only cards, available at post offices, VVV and GWK offices, and tobacco shops for €5, €10 and €20.

COUNTRY & CITY CODES

The country code for the Netherlands is ☎ 31 and the Amsterdam area code is ☎ 020 (leave off the 0 when dialling from abroad). Mobile numbers (which cost more to call) start with ☎ 06. Free information numbers start with ☎ 0800; those beginning with ☎ 0900 cost between €0.10 and €1.30 per minute. Directory inquiries are on ☎ 0900 80 08.

To call internationally from Amsterdam, dial ☎ 00 before the country code; to reach an operator, dial ☎ 0800 04 10.

TIPPING

Tipping isn't compulsory, but 5% to 10% in taxis is common. In restaurants, round up the total to the nearest €1 or €5 – a 10% tip is considered very generous. Hand money directly to the server, saying the total that you want to pay: 'Make it €40', for example. Toilet attendants expect €0.25 to €0.50, or whatever's posted. Doormen at clubs get €1 or €2 on your way out.

TOURIST INFORMATION

The main tourist information source, the **VVV** (Vereniging voor Vreemdelingenverkeer, Netherlands Tourism Board; ☎ 0900 400 40 40; ⌚ 9am-5pm Mon-Fri), is extremely helpful. It books hotel rooms and sells maps, discount passes and theatre tickets. Its information number is €0.40 a minute; from abroad call ☎ 020 551 25 25 (no extra charge). Offices, managed with the Amsterdam Tourism & Convention Board, include: **in front of Centraal Station** (Map pp38-9, E2; Stationsplein 10; ⌚ hotel bookings 9am-5pm, transport & ticket information 7am-9pm Mon-Fri, 8am-9pm Sat & Sun); **inside Centraal Station** (Map pp38-9, E2; Platform 2a; ⌚ 8am-7.45pm Mon-Sat, 9am-5pm Sun); and **Leidseplein** (Map pp82-3, B3; Leidseplein 1; ⌚ 9am-5pm Mon-Sat, 9am-5.15pm Sun). **Holland Tourist Information** (⌚ 7am-10pm), also VVV-run, is at Schiphol airport.

TRAVELLERS WITH DISABILITIES

Travellers with reduced mobility will find Amsterdam only moderately equipped to meet their needs. Most offices, museums, metro stations and public buildings have lifts and/or ramps and accessible toilets catering for those with disabilities. But many budget and midrange hotels are in old buildings with steep stairs and no lifts, and cobblestone streets are rough for wheelchairs. Restaurants tend to be on ground floors, though 'ground' sometimes includes a few steps. People with a disability get discounts on public transport; tram lines 1, 5, 13, 17 and 26 run wheelchair-accessible carriages, and all buses are accessible, as are metro stations. This book's listings include the 🚹 icon only where both entrance and toilets are accessible. The Uitburo (boxed text, p93) and the VVV (left) can provide details regarding access to entertainment venues and museums. More questions? Contact the **Stichting Gehandicapten Overleg Amsterdam** (SGOA, Amsterdam Forum for the Disabled; ☎ 577 79 55; www.sgoa.nl, in Dutch; Plantage Middenlaan 141).

NOTES

>INDEX

See also separate subindexes for See (p188), Shop (p189), Eat (p190), Drink (p191) and Play (p192).

000 map pages

SEE

000 map pages

🍴 EAT

000 map pages

INDEX